Who Am I Now That He Is Not Here?

ISBN: 979-8-9885943-0-7

Acknowledgment

Our collective thanks to the many friends and brothers and sisters in Christ who helped us bring this book to fruition. Each of our families has given us unwavering support for which we are so grateful. All of the reviewing and rewriting that this group of unprofessional writers required could not have been accomplished without your help. Thank you!

Over everything and everyone, we give thanks to Jesus, our Lord and Savior.

To the King of the ages, immortal, invisible, the only God, be honor and glory forever and ever. 1 Timothy 1:17

Table of Contents

Foreword

When we are about to venture into unknown territory, it is helpful and comforting to know what others have experienced who have gone before us. These beautiful women who have shared stories did not find much written about their unique positions as wives of ministers and missionaries to help them when they suddenly found themselves in unknown territory. Sharon, not knowing what it is like to have grass grow under her feet, decided a book like this was needed for other women in ministry. Much of their identity and passion was rooted in and lived out alongside their husbands. They each tell their stories of their journeys and of who they found inside themselves as the Lord led them into some familiar and unfamiliar places and passions after the loss of their life partners. Read and be blessed by their stories. Your journey is your own, but it is their prayer that by reading about their journeys, you will know you are not alone.

Beth Ann Contreras,
MMFT, LMFT-S, LPC-S

When we think of grief, most of us think of sadness, pain, and endings. In the following stories, you will find grief but also joy, appreciation, and wonderful memories that beg to be shared. A life might be forgotten quickly, but a legacy stands for generations. The men in these stories have left a legacy that can only be understood by the life they lived in service to the Lord. The stories shared by these women tell of the transition from serving the Lord with a life partner to finding themselves alone and questioning, "What next?". To some, this might feel broken and incomplete, but to the authors, the hope is that you will find encouragement and rejuvenation of what is next for the legacy you will leave, just as they also continue to live out the legacy they hope to leave behind, to the glory of God.

Judy Taylor,
MMFT, LMFT-Associate

Introduction

For many years, I have juggled a lot of roles, as so many of you have. Among working a full-time job, a full-time ministry, and a family of 4 – then eight as they married – and then 14 grandkids, it seems like there's hardly time to turn around. When COVID hit, everyone's lives changed in some way. Such a difficult time brought us all to see life in a different way. Enrique, my husband, and I have long been some of the technologically challenged, but we learned to transmit Bible studies and sermons, worship, and children's classes. And we were together.

September of 2020 changed our lives even more. You'll have to read the book to see why! Shortly after Enrique's departure for glory, the Lord laid on my heart the need to reach out to my fellow sisters in Christ. When you are the wife of a preacher or a missionary or any other servant of the Lord Jesus Christ and your spouse is gone, oftentimes, you are left in limbo. As Christian women, we have many roles and functions, but in the world of servants of God, many of those roles and functions are in conjunction with our husbands. When they are gone, we are lost (it seems). What do I do now? What is my role in my church, the ministry, with our supporters?

Now that I am part of a different society called widowhood, I see women who recognize their gifts and continue serving, perhaps in a different way. Others seem to wither on the vine, feeling that they no longer have a place. Churches often do not know what to do with these ladies. A preacher will be brought in who generally brings a wife with him. It's disconcerting for the congregation — to whom do they go when they need to find the communion cups? Who makes the roster for the nursery? Who leads the women's ministry? Do we put the old preacher's wife out to pasture? Do we invite her to go somewhere else? If she is a missionary, surely we don't need to continue supporting her when her husband is gone!

So many issues! Each case is different, but as the Body of Christ, we are called to do many things, and if we respond as Christ would respond, I believe widows will find their place, will continue serving, and will continue using the gifts they know they have – and even discover that they have other Spirit-given gifts.

The need to reach our lost world and proclaim the soul-saving gift of salvation is real. We don't want to leave any soldier fallen on the battlefield! Especially those who know how to fight!

So, as the Lord kept at me and brought up time and again a book for widows of His servants, and as I met more and more widows and heard their stories, I felt that it would be important to include several of them. What a wonderful team the Lord has put together in the ladies who share their stories in this book! Our prayer is that our readers, whether they are widows, families of widows, or church leaders, will realize the gold mine that is in so many of these women. This gold has been through the fire, has been refined, and is useful for the Kingdom.

This is not a book about grief, although we have all been through it or continue going through it. Our faith in the promises of our Lord and Savior allows us to see beyond the grief – and beyond this life. 1 Thessalonians 4:13, 14 tells us: *But we do not want you to be uninformed, brothers, about those who are asleep, that you may not grieve as others do who have no hope. For since we believe that Jesus died and rose again, even so, through Jesus, God will bring with him those who have fallen asleep.* And in 2 Thessalonians 2:15 – 17: *So then, brothers, stand firm and hold to the traditions that you were taught by us, either by our spoken word or by our letter. Now, may our Lord Jesus Christ himself and God our Father, who loved us and gave us eternal comfort and good hope through grace, comfort your hearts and establish them in every good work and word.*

There will probably be tears and laughter as you go through this book. May the God of all understanding, love, and wisdom bring joy and thoughtfulness to you in the reading of *Who Am I Now That He Is No Longer Here?*

May God bless you in whatever station of life you find yourself.

Sharon Bump Meza

Who Am I Now That He Is Not Here?

Chapter – 1
Who Am I Now That He's Not Here?
by Sharon Bump Meza

The charismatic young man with long hair and dark glasses watched as the *güerita* (fair-skinned girl) climbed the stairs going into Miss Carolina's classroom, certain that he would one day marry her. Never mind that they had never been introduced. Never mind that his lifestyle was on the opposite end of the spectrum from hers. Never mind that there was no chance in this world that her parents would ever even allow an orphan who spent most of his days on the streets buying, selling, and using drugs to form a relationship or would ever, ever be in agreement with such an arrangement.

But God entered into the picture and began working miracles as big as the parting of the Red Sea. The collision of the two worlds involving this young man and his *Güerita* would affect many lives in two different countries.

I was born in Miami—not Florida, but Oklahoma — on October 12, 1956. I was born to two young kids, Freeman and Carolyn Bump, 20 and 19, who were attending Ozark Bible College in Joplin, Missouri. They hadn't been in school very long when my daddy started preaching in Grenola, KS, and after attending a National Missionary Convention and meeting Wayne Hayes, they began dreaming of going to Mexico as missionaries. My dad is not one to spend much time dreaming—he just gets to doing— (hmm...I know where some of those genes have shown up!). He spent the summer of 1959 in Central Mexico and then came back and let my mom know that they were moving down to Salinas, San Luis Potosí. I'm sure those were welcome words for a mother of a 3-year-old, an 18-month-old, and pregnant with a third child!

Move they did in January of 1960 and lived for the first few months in a 14-ft. trailer with no electricity or running water. While Daddy went out on a bicycle, burro, horse, or car to save the lost souls of San Luis Potosí and Zacatecas, learning and perfecting his Spanish on the way, Mom stayed home. She learned to get water from the well and boil it for drinking, go to the market for meat before too many flies got to it, and wash tubs of diapers by hand. My job as the social butterfly who picked up Spanish by playing all around the neighborhood was to be her interpreter. I have kept that job all my life! The happenings while the young Bump family was in Central Mexico are just waiting for the book to be written, hopefully soon!

In March of 1961, we moved to the capital city of the big state of Chihuahua, where my two younger sisters, Susie and Judy, were born. The Bump family of seven was complete with four girls and one boy (and Paul David was more than what the girls could handle). Several years later, my dad's health and the need for us to learn better English and receive our schooling (I was home-schooled for the first two years and, I am sure, ruined my mother's desire to teach any more kids at home) sent us back to the States. In 1965, after a year in New Mexico, my dad was invited to join Bill Morgan in El Paso, Texas, to work with the newly formed Ministry of Spanish-American Evangelism (SAE), a ministry that, to this day, is a central part of our family's mission work.

My dad's love for radio and his remarkable Spanish landed him the job of preaching for radio audiences all over Mexico and into the United States as SAE launched their ministries that involved taking the gospel to the ends of the world through radio, the printing of tracts and Bible correspondence courses, and planting churches. One of the many letters they received was from someone who complimented them on the radio program but advised getting the *gringo* that gave the announcements off the program. The *gringo* was actually a Mexican national, and the preacher was my dad! It was 56 years later that my dad found, through social media, that a church had been established in the state of Coahuila as a direct result of this ministry. He recalled how the mission secretaries had told him that they had been receiving a number of letters from the same village, Minas de Barroterán, Coahuila. He decided to make a trip down to Coahuila and find this village. He stopped in the town of Nueva Rosita and picked up an elder of the church there. Together, they made a visit to evangelize more fully those students of the correspondence course, and now know that a church was established and is still going strong. The Lord's Word does not return void.

Who Am I Now That He Is Not Here?

His work in planting churches took us across the border to Ciudad Juárez, Chihuahua, a twin city with El Paso. While my dad evangelized in every colony he could get into, my mom supported the efforts by keeping the home fire burning and being by his side in the homes and churches where the gospel was being preached. Her beautiful singing voice, creativity in art and writing, and joyful teaching supplemented my dad's evangelistic preaching and teaching. I was always thrilled to hear them singing together—my dad's booming voice and mom's beautiful alto harmonizing. By the age of 11, I joined the team by leading singing and teaching kids, sometimes my own age. I have always loved to sing, and despite not having the best voice in my family, I do believe that one of my gifts is the ability to lead others in worshiping our Almighty God. However, my beginnings as a teacher did not have as pure a motive. I just hated it when the coloring pages were handed out; coloring was just not my cup of tea. Realizing that the teacher did not have to color gave me the impetus needed for me to take on that role. I am glad that the Lord did work on my heart, and even though I never learned to like to color (my sister, Beth Ann, still has her own coloring books), I am happy to say that a love of teaching did develop. And, with my having always been a ham, my love of acting has always helped as I many times prefer acting out a story rather than sitting down and teaching.

When I was eight, my dad and I were at Guadalupe Christian Camp. I do not recall if the rest of the family was there or not. But I remember that while he answered questions for my newfound friend, Holly, about becoming a Christian, there was an overwhelming desire in me to accept Jesus Christ as my Savior. I just knew that I was the biggest sinner in the world, and if Jesus came back that day, he would not be taking me with Him! As we all sang "Turn Your Eyes Upon Jesus," I walked up to the front and, before all, declared that I believed that Jesus was the Christ, the Son of the Living God.

My teenage years found me living in two worlds. My school life in El Paso was one world, but the one I saw as my real world was across the border. During the day, I very much enjoyed the social aspect of school, especially drama, and sometimes I even studied! But evenings and weekends would find me in very different activities. I was never happier than when we were walking the dusty streets of Juárez, evangelizing, handing out tracts or flyers for an event, or being in Bible studies in homes, many with no heat or electricity. I didn't care if they threw water or rocks at us or sicced the dogs on us. While my mom for many years had been the teacher for the children as my dad taught adults, my sister, Beth Ann, and I began taking on the role of teaching more and more (which did not put mom out of a job — it simply allowed her to teach other classes and do other things for the ministry).

At the age of 18, again at camp, this time in Jiménez, Chihuahua, I gave my life to serving Christ. I have never regretted that decision, nor would I ever renege on my promise to Him.

One of my favorite ministries was Vacation Bible School. My mom, my sisters, and I would sit around the kitchen table and work on putting together the programs for VBS. We translated songs, practiced with puppets, and worked on coloring pages and worksheets. Daddy had commissioned a tent made from sugar sacks that served as our shade. Our benches were long boards set on top of cement blocks. When it came time for coloring, the kids (usually more than 100 in each neighborhood that we went to) sat on rocks or on the ground. From the time I was 18 years old, I directed schools in Juárez, one summer holding eleven schools in three weeks. It was exhausting but exciting!

At this point, it probably sounds like I was the perfect daughter, missionary, and teenager, which is far from the truth. I don't know how my parents put up with all my dramatics, arguing with siblings, and the endless string of boyfriends that were around that *gringa* and her sister. Maybe they needed me on the team! Or maybe they were able to look through all that immaturity and rebelliousness like the Lord did and muster up their patience while I went through those phases.

Enrique's Story

It was during those teenage years that Enrique Meza entered the picture. This is his story: Enrique came from a family of seven siblings, the oldest boy after two sisters. When he was 12, his mother died suddenly at the young age of 41. Amalia was a hardworking single mother after having gone through a divorce from Enrique's father because of his physical abuse of her. An accountant by trade, she had provided well for her children, but her necessary absence from her children for work put a lot of burden on the older kids. After her death, the children went to live with their maternal grandmother, where they were not especially well received, but their pensions from Social Security were welcome, as were Amalia's assets, which included two houses. When an uncle was put in jail for fraud, Grandma did not hesitate to sell one of the houses to pay for his legal costs.

It didn't take long for the three oldest, Judith, Martha, and Enrique, to make the decision that they were better off on their own. So, at ages 15, 13, and 12, they moved into the remaining house. The girls continued their schooling in secretarial school, and the four older children began working to support the household and pay off the mortgage on the house. Enrique and his brother Carlos sold newspapers, limes, and other things but made the most money being altar boys at the local Catholic church. When there were weddings, baptisms, or confirmations, they made a lot of money from tips the parishioners gave them.

Enrique saw his role as the protector of the family and decided that he could best serve in that capacity by being a big man on the streets. His family and he had been instructed in the Catholic faith, and besides his duties as an altar boy, he had progressed to helping the priests in reading the rosary and other liturgical readings. He was mentored by one fatherly and kind priest, Hugo Blanco, but by the age of 13 or 14, he was involved in buying, selling, and using drugs. And no one messed with his brothers or sisters. His cocky demeanor and self-confidence quickly made him well-known throughout Juárez and the country of Mexico. His network of contacts was so extensive that the federal and state judicial police were constantly trying to recruit him to work for them. He would often state that he knew the best jails in Mexico! No one could ingest more pills or had such an insatiable appetite for drugs than Meza, and no one was quicker to respond to a fight or argument than he. His intelligence, knowledge, and bravado were widely known and grudgingly appreciated by those who surrounded him. His tolerance for drugs built up to the point that he was using heroin. One of his friends, being a chemist, knew just how to mix the right combination of pills to get the greatest high.

It was a life of degradation, filled with little responsibility and much sin. The coming together of young men and women brought out in them a life reflected in Romans 1:21-25: *For although they knew God, they did not honor him as God or give thanks to him, but they became futile in their thinking, and their foolish hearts were darkened. Claiming to be wise, they became fools and exchanged the glory of the immortal God for images resembling mortal man and birds and animals and creeping things. Therefore, God gave them up in the lusts of their hearts to impurity, to the dishonoring of their bodies among themselves, because they exchanged the truth about God for a lie and worshiped and served the creature rather than the Creator, who is blessed forever! Amen.*

His family and his friend, Father Blanco, despaired of Enrique's ever-changing despite his having lived through several drug overdoses.

But then Romans 1:16 and 17 happened. *For I am not ashamed of the gospel, for it is the power of God for salvation to everyone who believes, to the Jew first and also to the Greek. For in it, the righteousness of God is revealed from faith for faith, as it is written, "The righteous shall live by faith."* And what power there is in that Gospel!

Enrique's first encounters with the Bump family were at Crawford English Academy in El Paso, where Carolyn Bump taught for a couple of years. Father Blanco paid for his courses there, and often Enrique would watch that *güerita* (Sharon) when she would go to pick up her mom (called Miss by the students). And he knew that one day he would marry her.

Sometimes the tall *gringo* that spoke Spanish to all the students would go to pick up the "Miss" from the Academy. He was known as *hermano* (brother) Felipe -- well known to talk about Jesus to anyone who would let him. One of Miss Carolina's students, Filiberto, talked to her one day about one of his friends, Andrés. Andrés had been to the mountains of Oaxaca and had found God and wanted to know more about Him. Would she and her husband, *hermano* Felipe, go to talk to him? In all actuality, what Andrés had found were hallucinogenic mushrooms, but he, as well as some other boys in their neighborhood, began listening to this missionary couple. Enrique was not only a student at the same academy (paid for by his Catholic priest mentor), but he also lived in the same *barrio* (neighborhood) as Andrés.

The great interest shown by these young people led to the opening of a youth center near downtown Juárez in the early '70s. The days it was open were days filled with many young people who would come to listen to Bible studies and play games. But when Meza arrived, all seemed to wait for him to ask questions. They would give him their place in line at the only ping-pong table available. And allow him to always win! It was so frustrating to see their devotion to this rebellious character who was clearly the ringleader.

The messages brought by this *hermano* Felipe were just too simplistic to be true in Meza's eyes. They could not hold a candle to the Eastern religions and philosophies he was fond of spouting off about before leaving the scene to score another drug deal. *Hermano* Felipe would say, "If that kid would accept Christ, he would be a great influencer." For five years, we prayed for him. And *hermano* Felipe taught him, patiently answering his questions even when they did not make sense.

And then the day came. A revival meeting was being held in a packed church. At invitation time, the longhaired, generally high on drugs, Meza, stepped out into the aisle. He later told me that his friend Sar had pushed him out into the aisle, but Bro. Felipe saw him step forward and welcomed him with open arms. There was no turning back. As perverted as his life had become, Meza was a man whose words meant a lot. He had said he would accept Jesus as his Savior and had been baptized. The baptism took place on a windy February day in 1976 with the cold wind and dust blowing hard as he and others were lowered into the makeshift baptistery of a wooden frame covered with a canvas tarp that was outside the partially built walls of the church at Colonia Independencia #1.

After coming down from his drug-induced high and realizing what he had done, he put out a challenge to this new God. He asked God to reveal to him if He truly was what the *gringo* had been saying. He needed a job and a place to live, and he needed to be in school. By the end of that day, he had found a place to live and had a permanent job with the Federal Commission of Electricity. The director of the school he had been in saw him on the street and told him he was welcome to go back to school and to please go back—the first of many manifestations to him by the one and only true God.

For about a year, he stumbled along, leaving the hardcore drugs for lesser ones, leaving behind alcohol and his friends. Then he was gone. He went to the mountains on another vagabond trip to Oaxaca, Veracruz, and Mexico City. All the while reading the Bible. He started at the beginning of Genesis and found a God that destroyed whole cities and people. He found him to be very harsh and decided to go to the end, the book of Revelation, which was pretty scary! But then he found the Gospels and Jesus Christ. And he fell in love with Jesus. He returned and dedicated his life to serving his Lord and Savior. And never turned back.

Our Story

For five years, Enrique and I had been close friends despite his lifestyle. We spent many hours talking about everything under the sun and walking through parks and neighborhoods. After returning from his yearlong search to get to know the God of his salvation, we picked up our friendship. As our friendship developed into love for one another and our desire to serve the Lord increased, we both began seeing the need for ministry to young married couples. The youth group at the church in Colonia Galeana (the first church of many established in Juárez) was a large and active group, and many young people were a part of the new missions that were being established. But as the youth started getting married, we saw them leaving the church. They were no longer participants in the activities everyone else was involved in. They did not fit in with the "old" people. There was no place for them.

So, we decided it was time to get married. Someone had to take care of these couples! There was romance involved, of course, but we both had been very happy as young single adults. Neither one of us was in a hurry to get married. But the need was there, and the call was urgent.

On August 25, 1978, we were married. First in blue jeans at my parent's house in El Paso for our official ceremony and that evening at the church in Colonia Independencia #1 so that I could show off one of my mom's bridal creations and so our families, both by blood and in Christ, could witness the union.

18

By October, we were expecting our first baby, and our beautiful and tiny Miriam Sarai (Sita) was born on July 31, 1979. While I was still in the maternity clinic, Enrique arrived to tell me he had quit his job as a carpenter in a shop in El Paso and was starting his own business!

With his last salary of $125 U.S. dollars and borrowing my brother-in-law's, Enrique Contreras', machines, he started the first of his businesses. Although he was rarely without work, it was an uphill battle. Without capital and with the needs of a brand-new baby, we struggled financially. By this time, he and my dad had come to an arrangement, and Enrique was ministering to the church at Independencia. I'm not sure if my dad said, "Here's a church; you take care of this one while I start another one," or if Enrique said, "I can take care of this; why don't you go start another church?" Regardless, within a couple of months of being married, we were in charge of a congregation that had been running about 75-100 members. Soon, all the adults left, and what remained was a congregation of young people! But they, and we, were committed to the Lord and to the gospel. Thankfully, my dad's wisdom and prompting sent some of those adults back to us, but others who had been followers of *hermano* Felipe rather than Christ did not. It is a wonderful feeling to see that many of those young people who have stayed in the congregation to this day serve the Lord.

Three years after Sarai was born, we welcomed Judith Magdalena (Mags) on September 18, 1982. I was so worried about that little baby — how would we be able to love another child when we loved our little Sita so much?! Being the only little one of her age at church, she had been doted on all her life — and there were only two granddaughters at that time, so Nanny and Pawpaw didn't have to share their love with many! But that little Mags won everyone's heart with her dimpled smile and contagious laugh. It was then that I learned that one of the attributes of love is that the more you give, the more you have.

Challenges

But shortly after receiving the blessing that this little baby brought, there came a challenge that would last the next 38 years—a challenge that was not for the faint of heart. It was a challenge that would test and increase our faith.

In 1982, a devaluation of the peso occurred just a week after his banker had convinced Enrique that he should change his line of credit from pesos to dollars because the interest rate was so much better. His line of credit was increased so that we could purchase a furniture van. From one day to the next, we owed double the amount we had been lent. Within another week, we owed four times more. All of his suppliers and purchasers were in the same boat. We had a shop full of furniture that had been ordered but could not be paid for. We had bolts and bolts of upholstery material and thousands of feet of lumber that we now could not pay for. And a brand new baby.

Enrique began losing weight. His business of custom furniture and furniture that was sold to almost every furniture store in the city of Juárez would suffer to the point that we would have to sell everything we owned. Within a month, he had lost 50 pounds. In our ignorance, we did not recognize the classic symptoms of diabetes: weight loss, constant thirst, frequent urination, etc.

With my parents in the Yucatán Peninsula, we had gone to stay in their house. One morning, he was very weak and began vomiting blood. We knew he needed a hospital. We went outside only to find that our car had a flat tire. He was too weak to change it. I do not remember how that tire got changed. I suspect that my brother-in-law, Enrique, changed it because I had to take my two babies to my sister, Beth Ann, to watch while we went to a private clinic in Juárez. He was immediately put into a room with a glucose drip! That evening, I wearily went back to El Paso and my girls. Beth Ann was already taking care of her little one, and I will be eternally grateful to her for those days when she stretched her energies and food to help us out. Mags was only six weeks old at this time.

When I returned the next morning, I found a cardiologist in Enrique's room. He had finally done a glucose test and found that his glucose level was over 600. We had been to five different doctors during the month he was getting sick; not a single one had tested his glucose. I was instructed not to leave his bedside for 48 hours as he was likely to go into a coma. Enrique knew things were bad when his family started visiting—uncles and cousins who only gathered for weddings or funerals.

His testimony of those nine days was just the beginning of more to come. He felt his body going rigid and knew he was going to die. He made a pact with the Lord, promising to serve Him faithfully if He would allow him to see his little girls grow up. The Lord honored that pact, and he not only saw those little girls grow up but also their two brothers and his fourteen grandchildren!

In Mexico, where he was hospitalized, you pay as you go. I really didn't have anything much to do with his business, but with the help of Enrique's brother and the employees, I managed to deliver the furniture that had been promised and to sell some more, but I still didn't have enough to pay the bill. But God is good and provides for all our needs. One of our brothers in Christ, Rafael Burciaga (future father-in-law of two of my sisters, Susie and Judy), gave us the rest of the money to pay that bill. And so began the challenge of living with diabetes.

Who Am I Now That He Is Not Here?

We were thrilled when our son Steve was born, just 15 months after Mags, on Dec. 21, 1983. Just like our precious little girls, he was very healthy and welcomed into the Bump clan's growing numbers. But just as he was five weeks old (having babies was evidently not good for Enrique's health!), Enrique got sick again. This time, his intestines became paralyzed, and he couldn't digest anything, not even water. He was dying of malnutrition, and his gastroenterologist couldn't figure out the problem. He was hospitalized in the best hospital in Juárez, and exploratory surgery was performed. An abscess in his pancreas was discovered and drained, and while they were in there, his appendix and gallbladder were removed as well. He was sent home after we sold our property in Juárez and the machinery in the shop to pay for the bill. We were barely beginning to recover from his first hospitalization!

For two weeks, he was hospitalized and then sent home. A doctor friend of ours would go by daily to check on him and take him the medicines he so desperately needed. A nasogastric tube drained into a container that had to be emptied constantly. He was in so much pain. Back to the hospital we went, but this time they would not admit him. I had no more money to give them and no more assets to sell. When Dr. García, his gastroenterologist, found me in tears in the stairwell, he arranged for Enrique to be admitted and for us to make payments to the hospital—something that just did not happen!

Enrique was there a few days when Dr. García told me that Enrique was very, very sick and would need another operation. He suggested that I take him to El Paso. He probably should have gone by ambulance, but instead, White Lightning (my CB radio handle in the '70s) rushed him across the border. We went to the county hospital, where he was admitted for another two weeks. As they wheeled him into the operating room, the doctor came to me to let me know that I should be prepared for the worst; they didn't know if he would be able to withstand another operation. But the doctors didn't know of the pact between God and my husband. He pulled through and had a very painful recovery as they left his 10-inch-long incision open to heal from the inside out. The first surgery had been done horizontally; this one, vertically.

When the doctors there thought that he needed yet another surgery, we appealed to the Bump family doctor. He had Enrique moved to a different hospital and treated him there for another nine days, with no further operation. How in the world would we be able to pay all the thousands of dollars now owed? I don't know how it happened; it must have been a very astute social worker (and the Lord!) who filed documents for Enrique's bill — 100% of it for both hospitals to be paid by the Texas Workforce Commission!

His abuse of drugs no doubt contributed to these health problems, and his system needed much higher doses of pain medicine that the doctors were reluctant to give. What a difficult time! My babies were left with the nanny we had at the time and with Enrique's brother, Javier, while I worked a full-time job, went to the hospital, and nursed little Stevie in between rushing across the border to go to my full-time job.

Two months went by without Enrique being able to even have a sip of water. It was a red-letter day when the hospital allowed him to try some Jell-O!

Meanwhile, the congregation we were in charge of was being taken care of by the young people who had been so faithful, as well as my dad and other faithful friends like Carlos and Nelly Cásarez. Carlos was one of Enrique's childhood friends who had been taken up in the drug culture as well and had been rescued by the Lord. To this day, he and Nelly (who has her own story of family persecution because of Christ to tell) remain faithful servants and minister to one of the congregations in Juárez; what a powerful seed is sown by the faithful!

Within two weeks of Enrique's being released from the hospital in March of 1984 and with no more business to go back to in Juárez, one of his clients, a financial adviser in El Paso, asked Enrique to go to Odessa to help build up a trailer park in which he was involved. Enrique saw a lot of promise in that venture and convinced me that we should move there. He arranged for the church at Independencia to hire a preacher who had been at one of the churches in Juárez, and we packed up our pickup truck and our three kids, the truck piled high with all of our worldly goods. We looked like the Beverly Hillbillies or a scene from "The Grapes of Wrath" as we had no "black gold or Texas tea!" The normal five-hour trip to Odessa took us twelve hours! We arrived in Odessa and went to look for a church on Sunday afternoon. The only one open was one that we had been warned about by one of our missionary friends and by my boss for many years in the insurance agency not to go to! Bro. Bill Burr had told us that the church was so cold you could hang meat in the sanctuary!

Thankfully, that was no longer the case. Parker Heights Christian Church, with its truly amazing man-of-God minister, Paul Weymouth, and his elegant and kind wife, Barbara, were our saving grace. The church very graciously allowed us to use part of their facilities to have Bible studies in Spanish on Sundays (during the week, we held Bible studies in our home and others). During the worship service, we attended the English service, where the Spanish speakers sat on the balcony, and I interpreted Bro. Paul's sermons. It was such a privilege to be a part of that body. I loved being able to sing in their choir and learn their style of music. But even though we taught a good group, there were only two converts during our eighteen months there. Eighteen very long months!

So much happened in that year and a half. The Lord manifested Himself in many different ways. Even now, we are blessed by the time we were there.

On one occasion, Enrique went down to Juárez to bring back our very talented worship team from Independencia. About 12 of the team were coming back with Enrique, and I expected them to arrive sometime in the evening (this was the '80s — no cell phones). They did not arrive. All night long, I was sick with worry and prayed and called the highway patrol and hospitals along the way. It was a really cold night, although I don't remember what month it was. The weather in West Texas can be very harsh and changing. In the morning, Sita got up expecting to see her daddy and the kids from Juárez, but they weren't there. She asked where they were, and I could only say I didn't know. She advised me that we needed to pray. I told her I had been doing that, but she said, "Well, momma, we need to pray that they get here now." She bowed her five-year-old head and prayed. And five minutes later, they pulled up! We had a great weekend with them. The American church treated them like royalty and enjoyed their singing. I will never forget the faith of my little one — faith that continues to this day and that she teaches to her little ones.

On another occasion, we returned from a trip to Juárez to find that our pipes had frozen and burst, and we were without gas. What a mess! We did not have the money to pay for the gas; thank the Lord that insurance would pay for the repairs on the burst pipes. Our trailer had a fireplace, and we slept in front of it for several nights. Enrique was talking to one of our neighbors (a very incredulous neighbor) about the Lord when there was a knock on our door. It was some of the elders from Parker Heights. They told us that they didn't understand why, but they felt that the Lord was leading them to come to see us that evening. They prayed, and they left an envelope. It was $1,000! Teófilo, our neighbor, could not believe it! Maybe there was something to this faith business! We were able to turn on the gas and enjoy the heat again! It was a very difficult and cold winter. Enrique didn't have work. We often wondered what we were doing in that place, but there were rays of light — like our church family giving us money. As that money ran out, but the winter did not, we received a letter from some friends one day in the mail. It was from the Robinson Family. The Robinsons were a singing family whose ministry was to sing and play at truck stops. They had been given a contract with a tire company, and they wanted to send us their tithe, $2,500! That money took us through the winter. Enrique once again had work, and I began working full-time as well.

Even though we were frustrated with the lack of response to the Gospel, the Lord's plan had been fulfilled in the two converts, Juan Romero and his cousin, Uvaldo. The Lord's plan was not to continue in Odessa but in their ranch village of Francisco Primo de Verdad, Durango, a village more commonly known as Menores de Abajo — a village known for its violence and opposition to religion. Even the Catholic priest only went when he had to! Every group that had tried to evangelize or take their sect into the village had been run out.

But the Lord took Juan, a noted womanizer and feared pistol-carrying ex-soldier, and Uvaldo, his mild-mannered but highly respected cousin, and another man who had been in Wyoming and accepted Christ, into town at the same time. With fear and trembling, they first told their wives (who had a hard time believing in their conversion), then their families, and then the village. The Lord's church had begun. Land was donated, and a church building was built. What man could not carry out, the Lord did through unusual means.

The full story of Menores and the Romero family with their ties to the Mezas would take a book in itself. But suffice it to say that the Lord continues working on lives in this little village, and even now, a couple has been trained and has begun to work in the church in Menores that has been closed for about ten years. Juan's health has deteriorated considerably, but he will be a great help in establishing this young family in the village.

26

During the eighteen months we were in Odessa, we tried to make a trip back to Juárez each month. As the months went by, things were not looking good, and then we got word that the preacher that was there had begun teaching unsound doctrine. I thank the Lord for that faithful group of young people that had remained. They had been good students of the Word and could see the falling away from the Truth. They went to my dad, who very promptly went and asked (asked may not be the right word) the man and his family to leave.

It was during our time in Odessa that again Enrique was hospitalized, this time with ketoacidosis. Once again, I was told by the doctor that he was not expected to live. His glucose levels could not be controlled because the ketones were out of control, and they could not be controlled because his glucose was out of control. The doctor told me that he had never seen a person with his levels that was still alive — he should have already been dead. But that doctor did not know about the pact with God either! After three days in ICU, it was determined that he would need to be on insulin. This strong young man who was known for not being afraid of confronting anything or anyone just could not bring himself to put that little needle into his arm. The nurse training him gave him an orange to show him how he was to do the injections. It was so hard to watch him trembling to do that. But he faced it head-on and learned. From that time in 1984 on, he was insulin-dependent.

We returned to minister to the Independencia church in Juárez, and Enrique married several couples of faithful young people. It has been a joy to see their children grow and serve the Lord as their parents have. I Timothy 4:12 says: *Let no one despise you for your youth, but set the believers an example in speech, in conduct, in love, in faith, in purity.* It is certainly a Scripture to be held in high regard. It is easy to criticize our youth and despair of the coming generation(s). But we know that God is faithful and that he uses all generations for the spreading of the Gospel and the furtherance of His kingdom. We know that the Church is safe in His hands and that not even the very gates of hell will prevail against it (Matthew 16:18).

Enrique was a great student of the Word and studied many authors and theologians, comparing, questioning, and faithfully relying on his firm belief that the Word of God is truth. He could discuss anything from the metaphysical to the scientific to the theological foundations of many movements and was convinced we must remain true to the Bible, fulfilling the Lord's commandments. He was an excellent teacher and delighted in questioning and probing his students' minds and hearts. Sometimes, it would frustrate me no end to hear him repeating and repeating favorite verses or phrases, but now I am so glad he did! People remember his teachings. One of his favorite questions was, "What is faith?" Of course, Hebrews 11:1 *(Now faith is the assurance of things hoped for, the conviction of things not seen)* comes into our minds and mouths right away. He would invariably tell us to go beyond that, to delve further, to understand that faith goes beyond reason but does not ignore reason and that living a life of faith will prove the Lord's faithfulness over and over. His favorite classes were those where only the ones who wanted to go deeper into the Scriptures would attend. The classes would go on for four hours or more. Most of those students remain faithful to the Lord, and many serve as teachers themselves now.

He had learned from Bro. Paul Weymouth in Odessa to give titles to his sermons. His sense of humor often came out in the titles, and while we may not remember all the Scriptures given, the essence of the sermon on "The Incredible Hulk" or "What Cost God So Much We Cannot Cheapen" or "Who Would You Like to See go to Hell?" remain with us.

Both of our sons have inherited from their grandfather and their dad the gift of preaching and teaching — all four of them with very different but effective styles. Praise God for His Holy Spirit that trains and leads us! A lot of the training in our family came from sitting around the dinner table where the talk was not about football but about Christian truths, apologetics, doctrine, and theology. I thrill now to see my grandkids beginning to take part in these discussions!

Ah, but I digress from the history I should be giving.

After returning from Odessa, we picked up the ministry at Independencia, and Enrique once again began his business of creating custom furniture and doing remodeling/construction for factories, restaurants, and churches, with some residential work as well. They were busy days.

In 1987, our *pilón* (the extra handful of goods given in the market for free) came along. As I hit my 30th birthday, we did not have plans for another baby, thinking we were complete. But the Lord had other plans! Our Jonathan was born on May 4th and from the beginning was a handful! He was the orneriest of all our kids. There was no end to his antics. He made us laugh, cry, get frustrated, and thank God for him. He was the icing on the cake! Knowing that the Scriptures promise blessings when we teach our children in His way, we see that those blessings come to us many times over in our children and grandchildren.

Enrique expanded his business to include a line of southwest-style rustic furniture (that I thought would ruin his reputation) and began exporting to Santa Fe, New Mexico. I worked at a life insurance company as a Claims Manager and Administrative Vice President. We both had full-time jobs and a full-time ministry. As the kids grew up, they began working on the ministry team as well, teaching, singing, playing instruments, and evangelizing.

One of my favorite Scriptures is 3 John v. 4; *I have no greater joy than to hear that my children walk in truth.* God's Word taught to our

29

children will give fruit. One of these examples that I recall is when we all fanned out in the *Colonia* (a sub-division of the city) to evangelize and hand out gospel tracts. Steve was 12 or 13 years old and went with his partner to a home we had not been to before. The family in the home was of a sect that teaches false doctrine. As they prodded Steve with their false teachings, he was able to give them Scriptures that refuted what they were saying. While that exchange may not have made any difference in their hearts or understanding, it showed Steve, as Scripture after Scripture came to his mind, that the Holy Spirit indeed gives us the necessary words when we are called on to provide witness for the Lord (Luke 12:12- *for the Holy Spirit will teach you at that time what you should say).*

It was on a sales trip to Santa Fe, New Mexico, on Memorial Day weekend of 1997, that Enrique lost his sight. All had been fine when he went to bed, but the next morning, he woke up not being able to see. He spent the next couple of days in the hotel room, waiting to see if things would clear up. Down in El Paso, we had no idea of what was happening. (Remember, no cell phones!) On Monday, he drove himself down those 260 miles, guided by the white lines on the highway. Tuesday, we went to see an ophthalmologist, who sent us from his office across the street to a nephrologist. We didn't even know what a nephrologist was! (It's a kidney doctor.) The ophthalmologist had told us that his loss of sight was caused by diabetic retinopathy. The nephrologist told us that he had high blood pressure besides diabetes and that his kidneys were only functioning at 17%. Not only were they not functioning well, but they would not improve. Due to the grace of God and the talented Dr. Calderón, the ophthalmologist, Enrique regained his sight. Later on, he received more laser treatments that allowed him to retain excellent eyesight.

We began a close relationship with Dr. Raudales, the nephrologist. He was a very thorough doctor and managed Enrique's varied medical conditions very well. He advised us that Enrique would eventually have to go on dialysis or receive a kidney transplant. Talk about cold water in your face! How could this be happening? By the end of the year, Enrique was put on a waiting list for a kidney. Several of our brothers and sisters in Christ offered to donate a kidney for him, as did one of his brothers, but Enrique did not want to put anyone at risk.

During this time, we had opened our home to some friends of ours. The Álvarez family had come upon very difficult times. Sergio, Chela's husband and father of five, had lost his job and was also having health problems. They had lost their home and needed a place to store their furniture for three days. They didn't know where they would be staying, possibly at a relative's house. Of course, we told them that they could stay with us. The three days turned into nine months. Nine months of thirteen people (the majority of them teenagers) living in our four-bedroom home. All that long hair from six girls made for many plumbing problems during that time. Even though there were many challenges (pajama parties just can't go on for nine months — way too many hormones!), there were many blessings.

Neither Enrique nor Sergio was able to work, and Chela had never worked outside of the home. So, while I went to work Monday through Friday at Safe Mate Life Insurance Co., Enrique taught Sergio and Chela. It was like they had their own private Bible college. None of the family were Christians, but by the time our sojourn ended and they were able to get back on their feet, Sergio Chela and several of their kids had been baptized. They continued serving the Lord until Sergio's death some years later. Ministries are varied, and they don't always happen as we plan them. And the Lord provided for all our needs. That year was when I earned the highest salary in all my career and, due to changes in the company being sold, I was given two separate bonuses — one was a severance package of several month's salary, and the other was a package to stay while the company transitioned to the new owners. How providential! A family of 13 is not cheap to feed!

In June of 1998, Enrique got up to preach. His sermon lasted only five minutes (his normal sermons were an hour long on the short side, sometimes going up to two hours). He could not remember what he was going to say, and he couldn't recall the Scriptures. It was as if his notes had no meaning. His brain and his body were too full of toxins to make sense of anything. He physically could not stand. In our pictures of him from that time, he was like a skeleton. We knew that this was a turning point.

The next day, we went to see Dr. Raudales. He told us that Enrique could not wait any longer. He had to go on dialysis. Arrangements were begun for him to receive peritoneal dialysis at home. They placed a temporary port for him to receive hemodialysis in the meantime. We were made aware of the risks involved and the propensity for infections with peritoneal dialysis. And we prepared our home. A catheter was implanted in his abdomen, and we waited for that to heal. It was very difficult for him to even walk across a room as he had no stamina. The doctor asked us not to go to Juárez to avoid infections. At that time, we began helping a small Spanish congregation in El Paso, where the Álvarez family injected a lot of enthusiasm with their energy, activity, and ability to work with next to nothing. (They were in their own home by this time.) The church began to grow again, and Enrique taught as he was able. I taught the teenagers, and Chela began teaching children. Our kids would go to Juárez for part of the services and help at Logan Heights at other times. Even in this very difficult time, the Meza family served the Lord.

The day that boxes of solutions for dialysis arrived at our home, we realized that this would be major! We emptied out a closet for them to be put in and moved furniture around in the bedroom to make way for the machine. The time came to start. We had been trained on the procedure, and the catheter placement had healed. By this time, we were in late August. When that machine was turned on the first night, I just cried. Enrique had to lie very still, as any movement would cause the alarms to go off. The hoses would kink easily and had to be placed just right to drain into the sink in our bathroom. He was so sick. And I knew that I just couldn't raise our children alone. Here I was, an educated professional who could do so many things efficiently. But I just could not do life without Enrique. I poured out my heart to the Lord. He had always been our sustainer; I knew that. But these feelings of helplessness just wouldn't go away. I loved Enrique and would do anything I could for him. But I just couldn't seem to help any more than I already was.

The very next morning, I told him that I wanted to be tested to see if I could give him a kidney. He was too sick to protest. I made an appointment with Dr. Raudales, and he sent me to the transplant team. I filled out tons of paperwork, and then the day came when I gave blood to see if we would even be compatible; a lot of blood – fourteen tubes, I think (maybe more). Then we waited. And waited. And Enrique got sicker and sicker. I never knew when we would go to bed if that night would be his last. I praise the Lord for our wonderful kids. They held so many things together in our household and in the ministry during this time. They were not very old. Sarai was 19, Magdalen was 16, Steve was 15, and Jonathan was 11, and yet they carried a heavy burden. Each one of them has his/her own testimony to give about this time in their lives. I don't know if it was inertia, faith, or a strong sense of duty, but they all came through the ordeal with flying colors.

After waiting for several weeks for the results to come in on my blood tests, I was at my parents' home in the middle of the day, and, for some reason I do not recall, my parents and my sisters were all there. Even though cell phones were scarce at that time, I did have one due to my position at Safe Mate Life. As I was walking into the house, I received a phone call from the transplant center. We were a match! These two very different people – different in every way imaginable, but one in Christ – would now share even more. What a great thing to be able to share with my family! So many had been praying for Enrique, and our family was united in those prayers. What a glorious day! What a powerful God!

Even though we were a match, I still had to go through more tests — cardiologist, thorough physical exam, and other tests. And the final one was with the psychologist. She grilled Enrique and me. Had we thought of the consequences? Had we thought what would happen if I were to need both my kidneys? Had we thought of our children, what if there were complications? Had we thought about our own future as a couple, what if we divorced?

When I told her that if it hadn't been the Lord's will for this transplant to happen, He would not have allowed us to be a match, she responded by telling me that she had noticed that people of faith often had that type of response. I wanted to say, "You think?" But I held my tongue. Romans 8:28 has always been a favorite Scripture of mine (it was the Scripture that I had asked to be read at my graduation from El Paso Christian College years before). *And we know that for those who love God, all things work together for good, for those who are called according to His purpose.* And through all this, we knew that all things would work together for good as we did love the Lord and had been called according to His purpose.

Everything was in place, and the surgery was scheduled for October 9, 1998. Early that week, I was at a trade convention in San Antonio for business. The new owners of Safe Mate Life had been advised of the pending transplant and knew I would be out for a couple of weeks. I had been asked to stay on with the new company and had been given my title and salary. While it was a step-down, we wouldn't suffer any financially. All was good. Then we saw, coming in the door of the convention center, two of the managers. One was "the hatchet man." They took me aside and fired me. Just like that. How very heartless, I thought! They very generously said they would give me a severance package and pay my insurance for several months.

And then what? There were not that many insurance companies in El Paso, Texas!

I was devastated. The other two that were with me, Bill Yung, the Executive VP from Safe Mate, and Don Davis, who had left Safe Mate to become an agent for the new owners, were very sympathetic and supportive. They had been such wonderful mentors for me and had taught me much about our business.

Somehow, I made it through the day and returned to El Paso with so many emotions. The transplant was scheduled for that Friday. On Thursday, while Enrique and I underwent even more tests, I called an attorney. I explained what had happened. He listened very attentively and told me that, in his opinion, I had a case for wrongful termination. But then the Lord spoke through him. He was a Christian man and told me to think about it and put it in God's hands. I needed to be focused on the transplant. If I still felt like I should go ahead with a lawsuit, we would commence. I sat back down in the waiting room and opened my Bible. To this day, I cannot remember what Psalm I read, but I do know that it was one of the ones that asked the Lord to "take vengeance upon my enemies." I wasn't feeling very Christ-like at that moment! The Lord took care of everything. To this day, Don Davis and I work together. The company that bought us out only survived a couple of years. We still represent many of the same clients, and even though we have gone through many struggles, the Lord has never left us. Praise God for godly men who work in business!

October 9, 1998, the day of the transplant, after praying together, we were taken to separate operating rooms. Outside, our family prayed and waited. As Dr. Lozano removed my left kidney, Dr. Díaz-Luna, with Dr. Raudales assisting, prepared Enrique. Dr. Díaz-Luna told us later that he knew immediately that the transplant was a success as he saw the kidney placed into Enrique "pink up." We were taken into recovery and later placed in separate rooms. I could not eat anything after the surgery due to nausea. But Enrique took a meal, finished it, and then went to my room and finished mine! For many months, he hadn't been able to eat much of anything. It was great to see him eating that food with so much relish!

The next two weeks were critical, and Enrique had to go to the transplant center daily for blood work (he soon began calling the nurses "vampires"). My mother has always been on hand to help in any situation —whether it be baking cupcakes for a school or church party, making costumes for the many plays we did, writing monologues for me to learn, or babysitting. Now, even though she never liked to drive, she was serving as our chauffeur as I wasn't allowed to drive yet. Each day, she made the trek from East El Paso to Northeast, where our house was, to Central El Paso, where the hospital and transplant center were located. She made us so many meals and devised her famous "pockets" that my kids call Meza pockets, but they were actually her invention. She would roll out biscuit dough and put ham and cheese in the middle, topping it with another rolled-out biscuit and baking them. That way, Enrique could have breakfast after they did his blood work. We were at the transplant center for several hours each day as my mom patiently waited — reading, writing, or crocheting. My mom will have a very special place in heaven!

The congregation at Independencia #1 was progressing very well. It was a very active congregation, involved in the community and in evangelism through health fairs, Vacation Bible Schools, and revivals that were held in parks, patios, and in the street. We held VBS in the home we had bought in Juárez even before we moved in. The house no longer belongs to us but still belongs to the Lord as our daughter-in-law Ana's (Steve's wife) parents purchased it, and the community and the church are still served there.

The group of young people, including our kids, was an exceptional group. They were thinkers, and they questioned everything they were taught. They became devoted students of the Word. Out of that group, there are now dentists, lawyers, psychologists, medical professionals, business administrators, and entrepreneurs — all from a marginalized colony. Many of these kids became the first professionals in their families. And they served God. Many of them are still servants of our Almighty King. They carried on the traditions of the young people who stayed in the church when we began ministering. We cannot underestimate the power of youth! Among these kids were also many accomplished musicians and singers. It was a joy to be able to be able to sing with them! After finishing Sunday School and the morning service (two and a half hours), we would stay to practice while some of the ladies would take the little money we all scraped together to make a delicious lunch for us. We practiced until time for the evening service at 5:30. Enrique, in the meantime, would be in his office counseling a never-ending parade of people. The evening service lasted another two hours. After finishing up around 8:00 p.m., a large group of us would still go out to dinner together to our favorite (and cheap) *taquería*, El Cometa.

Around the time Mags was fourteen, a couple showed up one afternoon to check out the church. Verónica, the wife, says that her first impression was one of being taken aback by an American woman who came out smiling, wearing a Mexican shawl, that invited them in. Enrique began visiting with her husband, Francisco (Paco), while Verónica and I talked. They had shown up in a little, beat-up car that barely ran. At home, they had two daughters, Ana and Rebecca. They had just moved to Juárez and were looking for a place to worship. They had been sent to one of the large churches there, but they knew right away that they didn't fit in. It was a church that was full of higher-class people. People of society. Months before, that would have been their setting, but not now.

They had come from a city close to the capital of Mexico, where investments that Paco had made collapsed, as so much had, with a devaluation of the peso. Unfortunately, he had also invested for many other high-profile people, and even though he was exonerated of any wrongdoing, he and his family literally had to flee for their lives. They went from their important jobs (Paco was an investor; Verónica, a bank manager) and from having a chauffeur to take Ana to her private school to living in a poor colony of Juárez in a borrowed house, driving a beat-up old car. A brother-in-law set them up in a small business, and Paco started working for a supermarket chain in Juárez.

They had become Christians in their hometown but had not received the deep teaching that they soon found at Independencia. As Paco worked in the evenings, Verónica would take copious notes, ask many questions, and later teach him what she had learned. In a short time, they became valuable members of the ministry team of the church. This was the Lord putting into place what He was preparing for the furthering of His Kingdom.

Ana and Magdalen became fast friends, and (as I'm told) Ana began falling in love with Steve. She and Verónica would pray for the man that the Lord would prepare to be Ana's husband. Steve was pretty much oblivious to this as his world revolved more around the guitar than girls. But those prayers were heard, and in August of 2006, Ana was welcomed into our family as Steve was welcomed into hers. They make a marvelous team!

Among the questioners and thinkers at the church was a hard-working, extremely talented young man. He was older than most of the kids but had been much prayed over by the church and by his mother, who would constantly ask for prayers for her son, Armando. She and her other children attended church regularly, but Armando was too busy working or drinking. But again, the prayers were answered. Armando, who had dreamed of becoming a pilot, had given up his dreams so that his brother and sisters could continue their studies. Two graduated as orthodontists, and one as a business administrator. They were highly intelligent and did have scholarships, but schooling in Mexico is expensive and requires a lot of attention. Students do not have part-time jobs. They spend all their time involved in classes or schoolwork. But as Armando continued to attend services and ask questions, he began attending Enrique's Monday night classes (the ones that lasted four hours). He accepted Christ as his Savior, to everyone's great delight. Years later, he became our first son-in-law when he married our oldest daughter, Sarai (Sita), in June of 2001. He is still a deep thinker and surprises us all with his artistic creations — whether it be drawings (that have been in galleries in different cities) or t-shirts that he creates on his homemade machine. The Lord has used Sita's gentle and patient spirit to trim some of his rough edges!

When Enrique had been told he shouldn't go over to Juárez prior to his transplant, we had moved back over the border to El Paso to the house we had owned for several years. In the family meeting that we held in one of our favorite restaurants, we discussed this move, and one of the decisions made was that we would not take our long-time housekeeper/nanny/cook with us. Mari had been a member of our family for years by then. She remained in the house in Juárez where she would cook for the kids on the weekends and, to this day, is very close to us. Hers is another story that would make a good book – a story of conversion from idolatry and abuse to one of living a fulfilling life in Christ. Everyone was going to pitch in and help out to make up for not having Mari.

The newfound liberation from being hounded by Mari to keep their rooms clean (the kids were required to do their part) led Steve and Jon to blame each other for the messes in the bedroom they shared. The girls each had a room of their own. They decided that they would give up their rooms to Steve and Jon and share the boy's bedroom. They gave them six months.

At the end of the six months, with no improvement on the boys' part — each of their rooms was a mess — they took back their own rooms. For the few remaining months Sita and Mags were home they were back in their neat and orderly rooms, and the boys continued to share their mess. Such is the life of a large family! Once the girls were gone, though (Sita to get married, Mags to the Army), it was obvious who had taken up the slack of being without Mari. They are both much better cooks and housekeepers than I am. And the men of the house weren't even on the spectrum of housecleaning, washing, and cooking. They did take out the trash, though!

One of the hardest weeks of my life came when Sita got married and left home, and Mags went off to the Army within a few days! Sita and Armando are both very creative, and they have arranged things beautifully. Their cake was unusual in that it was on several different tiered stands, and each cake had a beautiful arrangement of natural flowers. With those and the flowers that decorated the church, we had a lot of flowers! The days after the wedding, the annual Pentecost revival was held, where each night, we would hold a service in a different church building (or outside since there were a lot of people). My mom took those flowers, and each night during the whole week, she would make a bouquet, taking out any wilted flowers. They lasted the whole revival.

As a senior in high school, Mags had decided that in order for her to study medicine, she would go into the Army and get her schooling paid for. I was so shocked that she would even consider going into the Army! We did not have any military in our family except my Uncle Tommy, who had been drafted during the Vietnam War (and I think he got out as soon as he could). The Army recruiter came to our house. We questioned him on a number of things, but what stood out in my mind was when I asked him what would happen to my daughter in case of war. He put a hand on my knee and said, "Oh, Mrs. Meza, we won't go to war. And even if we did, women aren't sent into combat." I did not know that they were allowed to lie. This was in April of 2001, just five months before the 9/11 attacks on the United States. Magdalen left just a few days after Sita's wedding.

While it was difficult for us to be without Mags as she was sent from South Carolina to San Antonio to Germany, we are grateful that the Lord placed in her life a young man, Nathaniel Taylor. We met him when they graduated from their training in San Antonio, and I naively believed that he was just her friend. Enrique saw right through them, though. I received a call one day, and Nathaniel came on the line. He told me that he wanted to marry my daughter! What? Since he could not communicate well with Enrique – being a through-and-through Yankee with no Spanish in his vocabulary at all, I had gotten the call. In no uncertain terms, I let them know that we didn't know him, and we didn't know his family; how could we give our consent to such a marriage? Magdalen told me that he was a Christian, and my firm answer was that anyone could say they were a Christian, but it didn't mean they were! Enrique and I suggested they wait a year and then decide if they still wanted to get married. I guess the next call was to Nathaniel's family, and they pretty much got the same response. They didn't know that girl and didn't know her family.

But they faithfully waited the year and were separated by many miles – she in Germany and he in North Carolina. Then, she needed an operation on her wrist. I could not go over there to take care of her. So, they cooked up a plan. We got a call one day, and the perfect solution, they thought, was to be married by an Army chaplain. That way, Nathaniel could care for her after her surgery. They could later have the wedding in Juárez. And that is how it happened. They were married in Germany on our wedding anniversary, August 25, 2003; then they had a beautiful wedding in Juárez in May of 2004. The Lord works things out so beautifully. We had a couple that was married the day after Mags and Nathaniel, and they used the same decorations and flower arrangements. And again, those flower arrangements were used in our Pentecost revival that year! That couple,

41

married the day after, is another one whose story would take up a book. Suffice it to say that Petra, a mother of two little girls who had been abused and then abandoned by her husband, had been rescued by the Lord. She married a man who had been a drunkard and a drug user who slept wherever the night found him but who had been transformed by the grace of God. This couple now leads and ministers to the church at Independencia.

Back to history: Enrique began his healing from the kidney transplant in October of 1998. Within a month, he was back in the pulpit and teaching, counseling, and ministering to the church. He truly did receive a new life with the kidney. He still tried to work in his contracting business, but it was very difficult; he just didn't have the same physical strength or stamina. What he did have was determination and a strong will. Philippians 4:13 was never far from his mind: *I can do all things through Christ which strengthens me.*

As far as my work life went, once Safe Mate Life Insurance was closed, Don Davis and I began working as agents for the new owners. Bill Yung, who had been the Executive VP, had decided to retire; he wanted to be able to speak more in churches and take more time with the Fellowship of Christian Athletes. Don, after leaving Safe Mate, began building up and adding products to Calger, Inc. Calger had been created as an agency to provide products to Safe Mate in order to provide more robust offerings for our credit union accounts. But now, instead of having assistants for everything and fancy titles (he had been Sr. Vice President; I was Administrative VP and Claims Manager), we were everything. Don hired a wonderful and hardworking assistant for the office, who worked with us until her untimely death. Since then, we have had great support in our office and in accounting, but Calger has pretty much been the Don-and-Sharon show for everything related to the agency and our clients. Calger has weathered many, many storms, and I am thankful for God's provision and Don's generosity. I have been blessed to work with many godly men, and I have always been allowed to continue working in our ministry alongside Enrique.

Most days before Enrique's transplant, he and I left the house early in the morning (the hour depended on which side of the border we were living on) and dropped the kids off at school. While I headed to the office, he met with clients or went to job sites or his shop. The evenings found me barely arriving at church in time with the kids in tow, and in the same business suit and heels I had put on in the morning and meeting up with Enrique, who was rushing in covered in sawdust or joint cement. We would sing, teach, counsel, and the next day continue on. While I think back and remember the long days (when we lived in El Paso, many nights we got home after midnight), my memories are of joyful service to our Lord. With the church in Juárez growing to so many congregations, there were always activities, not only at Independencia but with the other churches as well.

And then there were the summers! As soon as the students were let out of school (in early July), VBSs would start and would find the youth of the church and our family filling the church bus with chairs, tarps, and benches to head out to the neighborhoods where we would hold a school.

One of our memorable schools started out with some difficulty. Since the men, including Enrique, couldn't arrive until later in the evening, some of the ladies, the youth, and I set up in a park behind one of the church member's houses. This park was the dividing line for three separate gangs. I had taken some of the neighborhood kids from our colony (Acacias) with us. In my ignorance, I didn't realize that they had problems with one of the three gangs that saw the park as the dividing line of their territory. Before I knew it, they had used two of the little boys, one from each colony, to start a fight so that they would have an excuse to bring in the older boys. The Lord was watching over us, though. One of Enrique's employees lived in a house on the edge of the park. Chano came over to me and said he would escort the Acacia kids out of the colony while I talked to the others. I went over to the gang leader and told him that we weren't looking for any trouble. He was about 20 years old. I mentioned to him that we only wanted to teach his little brothers and sisters about the Lord. I don't remember any other words that I used, but I know they came from the Lord. Before long, we started our singing and teaching. The gang members were seated on the curb around the park, and I gave them a lesson as well. When it came time for the Kool-Aid and cookies, they helped us serve, cigarettes in their mouths and all!

That week, we had a lesson on the prodigal son. One of the kids, about 16 years old, called me over late in the week. He told me that the story we had taught had spoken to his heart. He had run away from his home in another city because his mother had taken up with another man and he didn't like his stepfather. He recognized that he had not been a good stepson either and was going home to ask forgiveness. I don't even remember his name, but the Lord does.

One of the gang leaders was called "Mono" (the word has several meanings, one being handsome, another meaning monkey). Mono was not very handsome. In fact, he looked and acted like the uncle in the Munster show! He had a shaved head on which he had the Virgin Mary tattooed. He was known to have killed several and to be heavily involved in many illicit activities. He was one of the ones who would sit on the curb and listen to the Bible stories. His little brother, Ángel (he was not), was interested in going to church with us the next Sunday. But when I went to pick him up in the church van, he came out and told me he couldn't go with me. The "Julia" (the police van) had come to pick up his mom because someone had told her that she was selling drugs, and he had to watch his little sister.

Years later, on a visit to Juárez, we were informed that Mono had accepted Christ as his Savior. After his conversion, the church where he became a Christian held a service there in the park, and, using a microphone, he announced to the colony that he had accepted Jesus as His Lord and Savior and wanted to apologize to the colony for all the wrongs he had committed. What a story of redemption!

We had the custom of holding revival meetings in this park after VBS at night. On Saturday and Sunday, one of the young men, who was a truck driver, would take a flatbed trailer over there with the church pews loaded up. They would be unloaded and afterward loaded back up and taken to the church. These are very heavy pews and took many strong men to move. On one occasion, as Alex was driving up to the park, a shooting between the rival gangs started up. He braked and put the semi in reverse. Our preacher for the week, Luis Vázquez, was at sister Emilia's house (one of the church members who lived by the park). They ducked down to avoid the bullets. After half an hour or so after the shooting had stopped, the pews were delivered, and we held the service. This shooting was unusual in that when we had activities in the park, they would halt the fighting. The president of the colony had asked Enrique to go see him one time. The police were there to thank him and the church and to let him know that when we were there, they didn't have as much work. Someone, I guess, hadn't gotten the memo that we were holding a service that Sunday!

On another occasion, our sons and some of the other young people had gone to play basketball at the park. Each contact with the gang members was an opportunity to evangelize them. The difference between the "church" boys and the gang members was very obvious just by their dress and demeanor. While they were playing, the police came and called our boys out. They began accusing them (of anything they could think of) and patting them down. Steve had just gotten paid and had money in his wallet. What the police wanted was money to let them go. But he had handed his wallet over to one of the girls, so they didn't find anything. The gang members then came up to the police and vouched for the clean-cut young men. They reluctantly let them go, seeing that they weren't going to get anything out of them!

Those were fun, exciting, and frenzied days with little physical rest. They were days that cemented our children's faith and desire to serve the Lord themselves. We could fill volumes with VBS, camp, and revival stories!

Our lives took a dramatic turn when, one day in the early fall of 2002, Enrique made a strange remark to me. He told me that he had been giving some thought to what one of our preacher friends, Samuel Guzmán, had told him. He had told Enrique that he should look into serving in a church in the United States — that they paid their preachers! There were several things strange about this remark. Enrique was very nationalistic, and leaving Mexico would never be anything I could imagine him doing. The church at Independencia was doing very well, so much so that we had begun discussing starting a new church in the downtown area of Juárez, as there were plenty of workers at the established congregation. All of our family ties, both his and mine, were in the El Paso/Juárez region. How could we leave them? I asked him when he had talked to Brother Samuel, and he responded, "Oh, a few years ago."!

The following week, my business travels took me to the Panhandle region of Texas. My custom when I was traveling during the week would be to find a local church to attend a mid-week Bible study. That Wednesday, I found myself in Amarillo, Texas. I called Roy Wheeler, who was the only preacher I knew there, to find out what time their service was. He informed me that they didn't have a mid-week Bible study, only groups that met in homes on different nights of the week. He suggested I try Washington Avenue Christian Church. I located the church and was surprised to see a banner on the outside wall. It advertised a bilingual Bible study.

I walked into the Bible study and saw around ten people listening to a *gringo* attempting to teach in Spanish. While it was difficult to understand him, his enthusiasm was clear. After the study was over, we introduced ourselves. When he found out who my parents were (he had heard of them but never met them), he said the oddest thing to me, "Would you and your husband like to come and work here?" Enrique's remark came back to my mind. The next sentence out of his mouth was, "Last night, we asked the Lord to send someone to us." Wow! In the four years that I had been working as an agent and going to the Panhandle, I had never been there on a Wednesday night.

Enrique and I went to Amarillo and met with some of the elders of the church and were invited to a meeting of the Panhandle Evangelistic Association, which was a group of area churches whose mission was to do church planting. It had been many years since they had planted a church, and now the opportunity was given to start a Hispanic congregation. In that meeting, they voted to invite us to work with Alan Morris in a church plant — and pay Enrique a salary!

The church at Independencia did not receive the news well. They said they would be happy if we were just there attending; they would do all the work. Enrique explained to the congregation that we were not needed there, but the gospel did need to be shared in other places, and the Lord was sending us to Amarillo, Texas. Things moved very quickly, and by January 2003, Enrique, Jonathan, and I were in Amarillo while Steve stayed behind for another year of schooling in El Paso (Ana may have had something to do with that as well!). The church at Independencia continued to thrive with Paco and the other elder, Neto, we had at the time at the helm. The story you will read in this book by Verónica Vega-Rodríguez will give you more insight into that period of time.

The first month or so that we were in Amarillo was challenging. We were used to a very active congregation and having a lot of people around. Now, on Sunday afternoons, it was only Jon, Enrique, and I in a small city with no one needing us or expecting us. No rehearsals for the evening service. No one was coming to our home. And, to top it off, Enrique was hospitalized just a little over a week after our arrival. We were renting a house that one of the brothers from Washington Avenue offered us. The house had been on the market for a long time, but he did not expect it would sell soon. Perhaps by the time we had sold our home in El Paso, we could find a place to buy in Amarillo. With Enrique in the hospital, I got a call from Bro. Scott said that the house had sold, and the new owners needed to occupy it in a few days.

Jon and I found a rental house nearby, and we rented that (very small) house for a year before the Lord provided the home that I still live in. Thankfully, most of the boxes hadn't been unpacked!

A very interesting thing that we learned in Amarillo was that we would not be dealing with Mexican people only. Amarillo is a city to which people from many different countries come. In the English classes that Enrique took at Amarillo College, there were fewer than 30 students in his class, but more than 20 countries were represented. Amarillo always has a lot of available work — hard work, which is the reason most of the people come! Besides Mexicans, we began dealing with Salvadorans, Guatemalans, Hondurans, Venezuelans, Cubans, etc. — every Spanish-speaking country. It was very interesting to see the differences in cultures. We had many laughs over misunderstandings of the usage of different words in these countries.

Washington Avenue Christian Church has a wonderful ministry of helping people with food and clothing. This ministry is called the Family Service Center. Bro. Alan Morris (the *gringo* giving the Bible study I attended) introduced us to this ministry, where we helped for over 15 years. While Bro. Alan had already been working with a small group, most of the people that we were able to meet and evangelize were as a result of this ministry.

We were able to make an interesting observation a few years after working there: those who received the Gospel and accepted Jesus Christ as Lord of their lives had complete transformations of those lives. The families that for years had frequented the FSC no longer had to go there; the Lord began filling their lives with blessings. Instead of needing food and clothing from a ministry, they were providing for others and sending donations to people in other places. Inversely, those who chose not to accept the Gospel continue to need assistance. There are so many stories that I could relate to about these conversions and transformed lives, but I will only tell you one.

Enrique had filled out the paperwork for two beautiful young ladies, both mothers of young children. One of them, Irasema, invited him to go to her house and tell her more about Jesus. When we went to her house, we found out more about her story. She was fed up with her alcoholic husband, Ray. The straw that broke the camel's back was the day that their six-year-old boy, Dilan, was to be released from the hospital. He had suffered a ruptured appendix and had been hospitalized for about ten days. They also had a baby girl, Ximena. It had been a very difficult time for them, and when Irasema contacted Ray to let him know that he could go pick them up at the hospital, he didn't show up for hours because he was drunk, so that was it. She kicked him out of the house. But Ray couldn't afford to rent a place of his own and pay for his family's house as well. So, Irasema, being a very practical girl, rented him a room in their trailer.

Their family was at this juncture when we began visiting them. Week after week, we went. After a couple of weeks, Ray would tell Irasema to ask Enrique about one thing or another. Then he started coming out of his room as we started to leave and would ask a question. Before we knew it, he was sitting at the kitchen table studying with us. Ray is a deep thinker and was raised in a very traditional Catholic family; many of his questions were comparing those traditions to this new teaching where only the Bible was being used. He had also come to the conclusion that he did not want to lose his family and was willing to do anything. So, he analyzed the situation and decided that he would start attending AA meetings. He was at the point where he needed to seek spiritual guidance. He decided that he would continue with the steps in the AA program, and then he would look more into Christianity. But after reading through Romans, he knew he just needed to accept Jesus Christ as his Savior.

Several weeks into their Bible studies, Irasema had asked us if we had a place where we could meet. She was surprised that we hadn't wanted to convince her right away to go to our church. We did invite them, and sometimes they would go, but never on time and not consistently. When Ray was baptized, Irasema told me that she just didn't feel anything — shouldn't she have some kind of revelation or something? I told her that she would know when it was time to accept Jesus. One Tuesday morning at 1:00 a.m., she called me. She said, "I need to be baptized." She had been reading the Bible, and the Lord spoke to her through His Word. I asked her if she wanted to be baptized that night (being raised by the evangelist Freeman Bump, it wouldn't have been the first late-night baptism I would be witness to!). She let me know that we could wait until the next evening when we would have a prayer meeting at our house. So, that Tuesday night, she was baptized in the big sunken tub that we had in our master bathroom. She joined about 20 others that used that tub as a baptistry. Jumping ahead to 2023, Ray is now the pastor of Iglesia Cristiana de Amarillo!

Being a part of the ministry of the church at Washington Avenue was a blessing. It is a congregation with many dedicated people and ministries. But we had been called to start a church, and we knew that as generous as the church was and as nice as its facilities were, it was time to become independent.

On August 21, 2004, Iglesia Cristiana de Amarillo was established. By this time, the Lord had provided for us a large house (with a great sunken tub to use as a baptistery), and we started meeting there. We came to have 50 in our living room and began looking for a place to meet. One month after starting the church, one of Enrique's classmates from English class and her husband took him to a location. The Núñez family had been given the keys to a warehouse where a portion had been prepared by still another church that hadn't taken off. So, we moved into the warehouse with the Scriptures in Spanish painted on the walls by people we didn't even know. We expanded into another part of the warehouse as our needs grew.

The Lord, by this time, had taught us that the ministry in the U.S. was far different from being in Mexico. We were not only dealing with different nationalities, but we were also dealing with 1st, 2nd, and 3rd generation Hispanics. We worked with a very transient population. It seemed that as soon as our attendance got up to 60 or 70, we would lose families. Then, new ones would come. It has been a never-ending cycle — but with a steady and dedicated nucleus. Talking through this issue, Enrique and I came to the conclusion that our main ministry here was to plant the seed and water it as much as we could: evangelizing, teaching people how to study the Word, and to recognize sound doctrine. We have had the privilege of continuing to nurture and counsel many who have been converted at ICA (as we fondly refer to the church) but have returned to their countries or gone on to other cities or other congregations.

The vision that was given to us from the beginning was to plant a scripturally sound, autonomous, central church that would support a range of ministries geared to winning souls for Christ in the Spanish-speaking community in Amarillo and the surrounding areas. I am happy to see that, almost 20 years later, ICA still maintains that vision and has expanded our local ministry to support several missions, which is unusual for a Hispanic church.

Enrique's kidney transplant had been very successful —never any signs of rejection (the marriage was made in heaven, after all). However, his uncontrolled diabetes and high blood pressure again affected his kidney. Our Christmas present in December of 2009 was his being put on hemodialysis. The Lord placed in our path excellent doctors in Amarillo, and, as difficult as dialysis is, they were very wise and caring. He would be a candidate for another transplant. The challenges again would be very great as we were more than 400 miles away from the transplant center in El Paso. The closest one to us was in Dallas, but the costs would have been prohibitive for travel and housing at that time since we had no one living there.

The transplant center in El Paso had relocated to a different hospital, but the same surgeon and nephrologist from the first transplant had developed an excellent and very dedicated team. He was put on the waiting list for a cadaveric donor. It was explained to us that a 2nd transplant would be very challenging (so, what else is new?); he would be more difficult to match and have a greater risk of rejection.

We waited for four and a half years. The dialysis was taking a great toll on him. The three days he went weekly, he had to come home and sit in the recliner for hours recovering, only getting up when it was time to go to Bible studies or prayer meetings. Enrique's dedication and will to serve his Lord were amazing and much to be admired. More than once, he stood up to preach, barely able to stand. Or, at times, his blood sugar would drop. There were several in the congregation who would recognize the signals if I wasn't in the service and would rush to get him a Coke to drink. He would drink it and continue preaching!

One weekday morning, the house was full as our daughter, Magdalen, and her family had come from Alaska, where they were stationed at the time. Many of our church family were here, as well as several of our kids. Then came "The Call." There was a kidney available! We had to get on the road within an hour. A prayer circle quickly formed, and then, while I got busy making phone calls, others started gathering things and packing for us. We had no idea how long we would be gone. We were on the road within an hour and made the seven-hour trip in six hours and 20 minutes. The kids and their families followed later on. We went directly to the hospital where Enrique would be dialyzed for what we prayed would be the last time ever. I was sent home that night, being told that the surgery would be early the next morning but to wait until I got a call to go to the hospital.

The next morning, the family and I that had filled my parent's home waited. And waited. By 9:00, I went on to the hospital. Enrique's room was full of doctors, nurses, and the director of the transplant clinic. Everyone was waiting. The kidney hadn't arrived, maybe in another half hour or so. Of course, everyone in our family and the church was waiting for word of what was happening, and they were praying. As many problems as social media can cause for some people, it was a wonderful tool for us in putting out updates. We were all so grateful that there was a great intern that summer working with my parents, Breanna Watt. She was such a jewel in helping out with all the grandkids that had descended on El Paso, Texas!

Finally, the nurse coordinator of the transplant team came rushing in, breathless. Sergio and his co-worker Isabel were wonderful to us during the process of waiting. In fact, Enrique had been the first patient enrolled in their new clinic (though not the first to receive a transplant). Isabel was a Christian; Sergio was of a different faith and was struggling in his marriage. Every time we saw him, we would share the gospel, and he eventually saw the hope in Jesus Christ. We were so thrilled after years of seeing him that he had accepted Christ as his Savior, as had his wife, and their marriage was now secure in the Lord!

But Sergio's job that morning had been very difficult. After calling us the day before with the good news, he had been told that the kidney would not be coming to Enrique. It was coming from Pennsylvania, and in their region, there were nine other patients ahead of him who were waiting for kidney and pancreas transplants. He had tried to persuade them and told them that we were already on our way. The next morning, he had made no headway and so was on his way to let everyone in the room know that the transplant was off. As he was leaving his office, the phone rang. It was Pennsylvania. The kidney was on its way! That was the beginning of many happenings with this transplant.

He was taken to surgery in the afternoon. The hours of waiting seemed interminable, but finally, Joe, the transplant director, went to tell me that all had gone well. After the additional tests were done on the donor kidney, it showed that Enrique was 100% compatible! We were told that the match was so complete that they could have been twins. There were still hurdles to get over, and as issues came up in the ICU, I would send out daily messages asking for prayers for his creatinine level, his blood sugar, or any number of things. After three days, the social worker came in to talk to us. She let us know that she was also a Christian but that many on their team were not, and they were being highly impacted by this transplant. She said, "As soon as something seems to go wrong, you tell us that everyone will pray for the problem. And it is solved." We serve an almighty and awesome God! The transplant was on June 27, 2013.

In August 2020, we got together for a cookout with several of Enrique's childhood friends. One of them, Carmen, is a respiratory therapist and a very fervent Christian. She told the group that she had something to tell us. Most of the group is not Christian. She began telling us of a nurse friend who had recently told her about a patient she had contact with who had received a kidney transplant. She went on and on about how there seemed to be many miracles that happened during that transplant and how their team had been so impacted by it. Carmen asked her if the patient was Enrique Meza. Horrified at the possibility of breaking HIPAA regulations, she did admit that, yes, it was Enrique Meza. Carmen praised the Lord in front of her and told her not to worry. She didn't divulge anything improperly, but she knew that patient; he was one of her best friends. Seven years afterward, the Lord was still getting the glory and honor for His great works!

Enrique had to stay in El Paso for several months as he recovered but was allowed to return to Amarillo for a weekend to attend a very delightful wedding. Raymundo and Irasema (the former alcoholic and his beautiful wife) had made the decision to follow the Lord correctly, so they needed to be married after living together for 13 years. Praise God for working on hearts and bringing them to His way of life!

Enrique was back in the pulpit on September 15, 2013. This book could go on for many chapters and pages regarding our family and the varied ministries we have been involved in, but that is not the main purpose here. It is important, however, that the overwhelming message relayed be that of God being in control of our lives and His church.

As the church matured and our sons became convicted to serve the Lord more fully, they were each sent in different directions. First, Steve and Ana had determined that he should study at Dallas Christian College. When they were told that their 2nd child would be born with spina bifida, it only served to make them more determined. They would continue with the plans and be in a city where our little *"Milagritos"* (little Miracle- Camila) could be taken care of. That would be another part of our lives that would take a book in itself. He was asked to minister to a Hispanic church while there, and even though it had not been his intention, he accepted and, for several years, served in Carrollton before moving to Cornerstone Christian Church. Cornerstone is one of those amazing and faithful churches that are very mission-minded and, without Steve knowing it, had been and is a faithful supporter of Bump's Mission to Mexico, my parent's mission. He now serves as Cornerstone's Senior Minister.

A few years later, I was asked to serve on the Board of Trustees of Spanish American Evangelistic Ministries. In my 2nd year on the board, I invited Jonathan to go to a meeting. By the next year, he was asked to serve as director. So now, he and Nadia – his beautiful wife and our designated prayer warrior -- and his family are back on the border, serving at SAEM and working with churches in Juárez. It's quite shocking for many to see the ornery little boy who was always in trouble now being the extremely capable director of this ministry that has been so crucial to the spreading of the Gospel in the Spanish-speaking world for over 50 years — the ministry that had initially taken the Bump family to the border. What an amazing God!

As of this writing, the Lord has now taken my daughter Magdalen and Nathaniel with their four children to Dallas as well. Their ministries involve taking care of others — Nathaniel as a Physician's Assistant, and Mags as a family therapist. They are very much involved in Cornerstone as well. And our faithful help in time of need are Sarai and Armando and their three precious girls, who have been our rescuers countless times, holding down the fort when we have been gone.

As the Lord continued to bring new families to ICA, Enrique's vision to train them more fully in the church became stronger and stronger. For years, he had invited Bible college professors to come to Amarillo to give seminars at a college level on many different topics. Most of our people are not college graduates, though some are. But those interested in learning the Scriptures more deeply would come and listen through the twelve hours of teaching over a weekend, oftentimes sacrificing days of work that brought them much-needed income. They have found that nothing done in the Lord's name goes in vain.

Enrique also spent many hours teaching one-on-one and in small groups. He could spend months on a very short passage of Scripture, wanting everyone to understand the essence of the Scriptures. It was frustrating at times to me (being a lot more superficial) to hear him repeat things over and over again. And now, I am so grateful for those repetitions as I hear so many repeat his very words that were drilled into their hearts and minds.

After having a wonderful weekend of camp over Labor Day weekend in September 2020, we returned refreshed and renewed to our service the following Sunday at ICA. After the service on September 14th, he called a meeting of the men who were part of the church. There were about ten men in that meeting. I had no idea what it was about, but afterward, he told me that his message to them had been that come January, he would no longer serve as the minister. He would continue being a mentor, but there were other things he needed to do. He was especially confident in the gifts and talents of three of those men: Ray Garcia, Noé Trejo, and Luis Zanabria. All three were students of the Scriptures and had different gifts. Luis had been part of us for about ten years and is Ray's brother-in-law. Noé and his beautiful family had been with us a shorter time, but he had proven to be a very faithful servant and an excellent administrator of the Lord's money given by ICA members. I was shocked and not just a little put out that he would consider telling them something like that without even consulting me. Talk about righteous indignation of his "helpmeet!"

That was the last Sunday he ever preached, the last Sunday he ever taught a class, the last Sunday he was in a full church service. The Lord gave Enrique a lot of discernment and foresight; I even think he had the gift of prophecy. Two occasions stand out in my mind. One of them was when we were young, healthy, and in love. He told me that he would not live past 65. The other time was in January 2020, when he told me that he would not be around much longer. I couldn't understand why he would say those things-either time. By 2020, we were so used to living each day knowing his health wasn't good but also knowing that God had special plans for him- we knew Enrique was one of His favorites!

I was out of town on business for the next two days. On September 17th, he told me he didn't feel well at all. Before the day was over, he was in the hospital. By the next day, he had a feeding tube in his stomach. He couldn't eat or drink anything at all. Nothing would go through his stomach. My mind raced back to 1984 when Steve was a baby and Enrique's intestines were paralyzed. Surely not again! For two weeks, so many tests were done. I lost count of the endoscopies they did on him. He never got COVID, but he was probably the most tested man in Texas.

Dr. Hendrick, his very talented and dedicated nephrologist, told us that they suspected cancer but couldn't locate anything. He believed that we needed to go somewhere else – like the Mayo Clinic. Nathaniel and Mags were now living in Phoenix and had always wondered why they were sent to a climate that they hated. Well, now we knew. We needed them to be there so that he could spend almost a month at the Mayo Clinic there. While Dr. Hendrick attempted to work things out where he could be admitted, we made our way down there. Normally, it was an 11-hour drive, but he couldn't make it without us stopping halfway there. What a nightmare to work with his medicines, the feeding tube, keeping him comfortable, and even getting him as far as the hotel room! He had no strength, and I seemed to be such a clumsy nurse. Our cries and pleas to the Lord were non-stop.

Once we arrived in Phoenix, we spent the night at the kids' house, but having no response yet from Dr. Hendrick and seeing Enrique so very sick, we went to the emergency room. He was admitted within an hour to the hospital, and we became part of the many, many patients that this research hospital is known for taking care of. They are truly a testament to dedicated physicians and staff members. After weeks of innumerable tests and very specialized endoscopies, the diagnosis did indeed come back as stomach cancer. I am so thankful for Nathaniel being available as our medical translator. The doctors would patiently wait for me to get him on the phone before they explained the results to us. What a devastating thing for someone like Enrique, who had always had such a zest for food – especially Mexican food and the fellowship surrounding the making and consumption of it!

By the beginning of November, we made our way back to Amarillo to begin the process of preparation for chemotherapy. There was even a question as to whether he was a candidate or not; he was so weak. From September through February, we were in the hospital each month, usually for two weeks at a time. All the while, COVID was going on around us. But, by the grace of God, I was able to be with him with each hospitalization except for one where the numbers of COVID had gone up so high that no one was allowed in. During those two nightmarish weeks, the kids and I had him on a Messenger call constantly, everyone taking their turn. Sita and Armando both worked night shifts so they could take over while the rest of us slept. He was in so much pain and had been given so much medication that he would hallucinate. The hospital placed a 24-hour sitter with him to keep an eye on him as he had become violent one of the days. And the prayers went up all over the place, even by those not known to us. When I was asked what they should pray for, I would tell them to pray for God's perfect will.

When not hospitalized, he would spend his hours in a recliner in our bedroom. And even though he was not able to go to church, he took calls constantly and taught and gave advice. And he received numerous calls from many that had caused him grief through the years. Some who didn't even know he was sick felt led to call him and ask for forgiveness. His grace came from the Lord; he never held a grudge against anyone who had harmed him or the Lord's work; he knew that the Lord was in control of it all. Very few times would he complain. He didn't complain about what he was going through, but at times, the pain was unbearable for him. We both learned from one of our professors not to ask "why" but to ask "what for" (which, truthfully, sounds much better in Spanish).

He underwent several sessions of chemotherapy and was scheduled for the removal of most or all of his stomach in early March. Our bedroom was a hospital room and pharmacy. I emptied a bookcase and first put all his medicines in alphabetical order, then in order of administration, but by the end of each day, it would be jumbled again depending on which need was greater. I had to get out my instructions, which were in a notebook, to make sure I was giving the correct medication at the correct time in the correct dosage. There were boxes and boxes of bags and tubes and the nutrition that had to be put in the tube. I had pill crushers and cutters, measuring utensils, and alarms set. Throughout the day and through the night, the alarm would go off on the machine with the feeding tube connected. Going out to doctors' appointments was a major undertaking, even though we had been given a backpack that was supposed to let Enrique move around with greater freedom.

Enrique was hospitalized again in mid-February, just as the worst winter storm of 2021 set in, and he asked me to read Romans 1 to him. I had just finished reading verses 16 and 17: *For I am not ashamed of the gospel, for it is the power of God for salvation to everyone who believes, to the Jew first and also to the Greek. For in it, the righteousness of God is revealed from faith for faith as it is written, "The righteous shall live by faith."* Just then, a young man, a nurse tech, came in and saw us reading the Word. He began sharing his testimony of faith as well. What a precious time of sharing we had! We fell asleep, and the next morning, I got up and went to the cafeteria for some breakfast. I came back to a room full of commotion. I had no idea what was going on. They were all from the Intensive Care Unit. I still don't know what prompted them to rush to his room.

Down in the ICU, the kind doctor who was on shift that day came to talk to me. She told me that Enrique would not last much longer but that they could put him on life support. I quickly called the kids. It was Sunday, and Steve was already at the church preparing to preach. We all listened to her explanation of his condition, and unanimously, we all told her that he was in God's hands. If the Lord wanted to work a miracle in his health, it would be done; it wouldn't be the first time. But if it was his time to be called to Glory, then he should be allowed to go. She excused herself; I hung up the call with the kids. In a few minutes, she returned and apologized to me. She said she had had to go cry. To see our oneness of mind was such a blessing to her. In the next room, there was a family whose mother would die that day, and they were tearing each other apart. How sad to not know what lies in your future!

Before I knew it, Sita was by my side, and Steve was preaching, knowing that's what his dad would have wanted. By that night, all the kids were there. Steve spent the night with him while I went home to rest, having spent the last few nights at the hospital.

The next morning, a nurse went in from hospice care and gave us our options. We asked if he could go home, and she said yes. By 4:00 p.m., we had a hospital bed in our room, the nurse was there, and Enrique was brought in. I gathered all 14 grandkids and explained to them that their grandpa would soon be with Jesus, but there was time for them to go talk to him if they wanted. The four older girls went in immediately, and I could hear them talking to Grandpa, telling him about Hannah's new boyfriend (to which Enrique reacted, scaring them all!). They laughed and cried, and then the boys and younger girls trooped in. For a long time, Enrique had called Seth (Jon's oldest) his "cane," which he really took to heart. He is still very sensitive in taking care of older people. Naomi stood up from our gathering and announced she was going outside to skate away her sadness. Fourteen different reactions, 14 young lives that no one thought he would ever see. Fourteen current and future servants of our Lord and King witnessing the triumph of a devoted man of God making his way to Glory.

That evening, our church started coming in to join the family. Forty or so made their way into our bedroom, where a time of worship and praise, praying, and reading of the Scripture flowed and surrounded us all. Enrique lay peacefully on the bed, no longer attached to any tubes. Nathaniel was ready to administer any medication he needed, but there was no need for that. And he was able to be at the side of his father-in-law for special moments that he hadn't been able to spend with his own parents at their passing. This beautiful scene went on and on. There were many tears, but there was laughter as well. By midnight, the last person had left. Luisa Trejo had stayed until the last passing moments with Enrique, who she always said reminded her so much of her own father, with whom she hadn't been able to be when he passed away. Mags stayed by his bedside when all was quiet and told me to lie down. As soon as I did, I fell into a deep sleep. Within fifteen minutes, she went to tell me that he was gone.

Jim Shelburne, the minister at Washington Avenue Christian Church, had made arrangements for us with a funeral home. One phone call got the nurse out to certify his death, and within an hour, he had been taken away, and the hospital bed was gone. The children were all asleep except Sarah, who watched her Grandpa leave home for the last time, but she knew that he already had a better home to go to.

The next morning, the parade of Christian brethren, not only from ICA but from other churches in town, began. Nadia's family brought in loads of water, fruit, bread, and I don't know what else. Others brought in pizza and other food. Loads of flowers and plants came from business associates, out-of-town families, and churches. I had no idea how we would ever eat so much food. But the Lord knew. That night, the house was once again filled with our church family, and we sang and praised, prayed, and read. And were comforted beyond any earthly comfort.

Brothers and sisters, we do not want you to be uninformed about those who sleep in death so that you do not grieve like the rest of mankind, who have no hope. For we believe that Jesus died and rose again, and so we believe that God will bring with Jesus those who have fallen asleep in him (I Thessalonians 4:13, 14).

The next day, the kids and I (mostly the kids) talked through his memorial service. Two days after he was called home, we held a service in a packed church (and no one got COVID). All my family was in attendance, having traveled from all over Texas and Oklahoma, as were so many of Enrique's minister friends from other churches and the members of ICA, past and present, as well as our dear and faithful brother and sister from Odessa where we had been so many years before, Paul and Barbara Weymouth, and other brothers and sisters in Christ from Colorado and Dallas. How humbling to see so many who cared about this man who had lived a life that left such a tremendous legacy! We had a wonderful time of celebration, at the end of which Jonathan made an announcement, "To all of you that have borrowed my dad's tools and books and haven't returned them, we have made an executive decision: you can keep them." There was a lot of laughter, as that was one of his pet peeves. We all sang, the boys played their instruments, and my sister Susie played the piano. Steve preached, and God was glorified.

From Amarillo, we made our way down to the border, where three additional memorial services were held. One at the church we ministered to for 24 years, Independencia #1, at Revolución Mexicana, where we had gone to serve for six months a few years prior when there was a lot of turmoil there (another book), and one at the SAEM (Spanish American Evangelistic Ministries) offices for those that could not cross the border. Enrique got quite a send-off!

We can all see how the Lord worked in Enrique's life and the testimony that his life continues to give. A life well lived, a conviction that never faltered, a diamond that was truly in the rough but became well-polished.

So, who am I now that he is not here?

And your ears shall hear a word behind you, saying, *"This is the way, walk in it," when you turn to the right or when you turn to the left* (Isaiah 30:21). As opportunities for continued and new ways of ministering come to me, I like to rely on that still, small voice of the Lord telling me which way to go. As much as I would like to audibly hear that voice all the time, it doesn't always happen. But the Lord has put wise counselors all around me. I am blessed to have godly parents still with me, as well as siblings, children, and a wonderful congregation with dedicated and wise leaders. Even my grandchildren get in on the act of helping me weigh options and opportunities. And I just love the group of dedicated and godly women who have come together with me to bring you our stories. Our prayer is that through seeing our different circumstances and lives, you will be encouraged to step up and into the ministries the Lord is leading you into.

I am still the eight-year-old in need of salvation; I am the 18-year-old dedicating her life to serving the Lord; I am the bride vowing to go where my husband would go, his people being my people, his God my God; I am a widow with the full knowledge that my beloved husband is rejoicing in Glory, much better off than here on earth; and I am happily looking forward to the day when Jesus comes again, or I go to meet Him. And I will go through those doors that open up to me where I can be of service to the King of kings and Lord of lords and to His glorious church. So, those days when memories of Enrique's and my life come flooding over me when I see him in the place he would stand to preach, or hear his voice on one of his recordings, or see a video of him playing with our grandchildren, I recall songs or scriptures that lift me up and put me and my mind back on course! One of those has been Psalms 144:1, 2:

Blessed be the Lord, my rock, who trains my hand for war, and my fingers for battle; he is my steadfast love and my fortress, my stronghold and my deliverer, my shield and he in whom I take refuge, who subdues people under me.

I will close with one of my favorite Scriptures, Habakkuk 3:17 – 19:

> *Though the fig tree should not blossom,*
> *nor fruit be on the vines,*
> *the produce of the olive fail*
> *and the fields yield no food,*
> *the flock be cut off from the fold*
> *and there be no herd in the stalls,*
> *yet I will rejoice in the LORD;*
> *I will take joy in the God of my salvation.*
> *GOD, the Lord, is my strength;*
> *he makes my feet like the deer's;*
> *he makes me tread on my high places.*

May the glory of the Lord shine on, in, and through you.

Chapter – 2
Born in Estado Grande by
Verónica Vega

I was born in Estado Grande, Chihuahua, Mexico and grew up in a small village of no more than 2,000 inhabitants buried in the mountains, Temósachic. I was the eighth of 11 siblings (10 girls and one boy) with a Tarahumara mother, strict and with great principles and values that she taught us from infancy.

I lived out my childhood in poverty but was very happy. We were all together, and that sufficed at my tender age. The Catholic religion was quite rooted in all the family. And, yes, I must admit that until I met Christ, I was a really good Catholic. Priests from different parts of the country and the world arrived at our village, some very strict in their doctrine and others quite liberal. Among them was a Spanish priest who became a friend to almost the whole village. It was then at my young age (nine or ten years) that I began asking myself questions related to the religion we practiced because, in his talks, he made us see things we were doing that were not right. I paid close attention to his sermons during mass and asked myself, "Why do we do things contrary to the Bible?" But when I asked an adult, the answer was, "You are here to obey and not to ask."

I was 14 when we left the village due to a sensitive situation involving my father. We migrated to the city of Pachuca, Hidalgo, Mexico, near Mexico City in the central part of Mexico. By then, only five siblings were still at home. So, with Mamá and Papá, we arrived at a great city full of buildings, vehicles, and people – a huge population with a lot of activity. Could one imagine what this meant to a 14-year-old adolescent?

Mamá immediately sought out the Catholic church closest to the area in which we lived. We caused quite a stir in the family because we girls had arrived from the north with different accents and customs. My brother-in-law's family was quite large and treated our family in a nice way, receiving us with much love and joy.

Among them was a handsome, dashing cousin of my brother-in-law, who impulsively and daringly began to court me without my parents' authorization, especially my mother's, as she was quite strict in her standards and obligations regarding her daughters. Nothing should happen before one is 15 years old. The time was close; I would be 15 in just a few months. How much did that matter? Stubbornly, he insisted and gained permission for me to be his girlfriend.

Who Am I Now That He Is Not Here?

We began a very healthy relationship. Why? I didn't know anything; I was naïve about everything. He was quite young, and I believe he was also naïve. So, we had a lovely, pure engagement supervised by my parents and family. He also was Catholic but more in name only.

We were engaged for several years, though we weren't always together because my family returned to Chihuahua after a time, and our relationship went through problems with the distance. Finally, after several years, our relationship improved, and he asked me to marry him. I said, "Yes," and we married on the Fourth of July.

We both worked; he, a graduate engineer, and I, a bank employee. We had a stable marriage with normal highs and lows, but we became more and more adapted to each other little by little.

We enjoyed the next months of our marriage, and in December, we learned that we would be parents. We rejoiced with this notice, and so did the whole family. We became new parents of a beautiful little girl who immediately conquered the whole family as she was one of the youngest granddaughters and daughter of the youngest son of a large family. My dear mother-in-law tended to me and took care of me like a daughter and also began helping us with our newborn because we both returned to work.

At this time, I had been given a new position where I worked that carried the great responsibility of dealing directly with corporations and branches of state government. Through an unusual situation, I found myself involved in an unpleasant situation that brought about great consequences in my personal life and, most importantly, in our married life, putting our general coexistence at high risk.

One of my dear sisters-in-law began to attend a church in the city, and when she saw our need, she began inviting us to meetings in her house. My husband, resistant to change, heartily opposed her. But I began to remember all I had heard and said to myself, "This is correct; it's in agreement with what the Bible says."

Finally, we agreed to attend a Sunday service, and my husband was immediately caught up. He was enthralled by the worship, and, if I remember correctly, only two or three Sundays went by when, at the invitation, he went forward to accept Christ. My husband was one of the first to go forward, and I followed him. That was one of the most beautiful experiences we had together. Romans 10:9 says, *"Because, if you confess with your mouth that Jesus is Lord and believe in your heart that God raised him from the dead, you will be saved."*

Our relationship improved 100% in all aspects, and almost immediately, we became involved in all the activities of the congregation. And so, we began our first ministry: CLEANING THE BATHROOMS OF THE CHURCH BUILDING. We did this for three years with enthusiasm, although I must say that nobody ever congratulated us on our good work. Nevertheless, this was just the beginning of our preparation for serving the Lord. We served with all our love and thanksgiving to our God. Without a doubt, He was preparing His servant, my husband, which could be seen in his desire to serve. Not everything went like we thought it would, but we were sure that God was with us.

We tried for several years to have another baby but didn't succeed. We went through treatments and situations of illness that made it difficult for me to become pregnant. After nine years, we finally learned that we would be parents again. At the end of the wait, we had our second daughter. The birth was difficult, and the doctor recommended that we not have another baby because my life was at risk. So, we had our two daughters who were ten years apart, and we were grateful and happy.

My husband began to prosper financially, but at the same time, his physical body began presenting some health problems. And just when it seemed that everything was going well in his business, the peso devaluation of 1995 hit, and we were left literally without anything. So, without wanting to, we migrated to the state of Chihuahua in northern Mexico to Ciudad Juárez with the help of one of my sisters and her husband (my beloved Morayma and Pablo), who lived in Albuquerque, New Mexico, in the U. S., and had property in Juárez, where my family arrived to live. It was a difficult process because we had to leave everything behind. And when I say everything, it was church, family, jobs, and all that could link us to that city. Then I could see how my husband, who was not accustomed to the climate, the customs, or the food, had to begin from nothing along with our daughters in that everything seemed odd and ugly to them. The people who brought us to Juárez, great friends and brethren in Christ, left us in charge of a church in the city, but to be honest, even though we tried hard, we couldn't fit in and ended up leaving the place determined to find a better place, according to us.

My husband, who was not accustomed to hard physical labor, began working in a supermarket business, where, on his first day, he washed an endless pile of bread trays. He had been hired for the bakery department. Every day, he arrived home with his hands literally bleeding from so much soap and water. But in spite of that, he was happy. He would say, "I feel like a real husband supplying my family's needs!" Though, to be honest, the pay wasn't much and barely provided the most basic needs of our family.

We had a very discreet relationship with our family in Pachuca; we only communicated with our angels, Mario and Irma (Paco's brother-in-law and sister). For a long time, they provided for our economic needs along with my sister Morayma and her husband, Pablo. In fact, even today, they still do, along with other family members: siblings, in-laws, nieces and nephews, and my beloved Coquito (my mother-in-law).

Again, we began seeking a church to meet with, and close to our family home, we found a church with which we met for about three months. But we noticed, and I say so with much respect, that their doctrine was not in accordance with the Scripture. (No earrings, no pants, no short hair, no makeup, men and women separated, head covered, etc.) So, again, we found ourselves without a place to meet.

My husband traveled to and from work on the bus that passed through our colony and dropped him off a few blocks from work. We didn't have a car, so all our traveling around was by bus. One thing we had kept from our church in Pachuca was some T-shirts printed with Bible verses that we took great care of. One day, as Paco was on his way to work, a man came up to him on the bus and said the verse on Paco's shirt had caught his attention and asked if he was a Christian. My husband answered affirmatively, and there on the bus, he received an invitation to the church where our beloved brother Pascual attended, which was just a few blocks from our house.

When my husband arrived home, he commented enthusiastically on what had happened. My warning was, "All right, but if it's another place like the one before, we won't stay there."

In all honesty, it had been several days that our cupboard was bare because our financial situation didn't allow for much, and we also had gotten an old car that we had to make payments on. We were in a discouraging situation. Even so, we took heart and went to find the church with the plan that if we saw the women like in the one before, we would leave immediately.

When we arrived at the place, there was a lot of commotion as they had a special event going on; if I remember right, it was a couples' meeting. The person who came out to meet us was a very talkative and kind woman, and, yes, she had on earrings and a little makeup. Joyfully, she invited us to

73

enter, but my excuse was that there were no children there. That didn't matter to her, and she insisted we enter into the event; above all, she informed us they had food. So, we accepted the invitation as we hadn't eaten well in several days, especially our daughters. When we went in, how wonderful it was to see a table full of different kinds of food! So, our instructions to our daughters were to eat all they could, and we would also. I don't remember the theme of the event or much about the other people there, but I do remember the beautiful table full of food. We stayed to hear the sermon. It was easier with full stomachs. But who was the woman God put in our path and was His instrument to make a difference in our life forever? It was our sister, friend, and co-mother-in-law (mother-in-law of one of our daughters), Sharon Meza. At the end of the event, a big man with rugged features, strict and bossy, came up to us; seeing him for the first time had a big impact on me. He took down the information he needed so as not to lose contact with us. He was the preacher, our friend, and our co-father-in-law, Enrique Meza. (Why do I say co-parents-in-law? Well, some years later, our older daughter married one of their sons.)

On our way home, we commented that all had gone well. The only thing that disturbed us a bit was the preacher, for he had seemed a little rude, strict, and bossy, but outside of that, all was good: a small church, close to our house, with nice people, that didn't prohibit anything, and with the doctrine that had seemed to come right from Scripture (to be honest, the doctrine and customs we had brought with us weren't the best). Our next visit to the church was one Wednesday for a Bible study and prayer meeting. When we arrived, there was a lady playing the piano, and we didn't know the songs as they were hymns. At the end of the service, the preacher came up to ask how we were feeling, and my husband's first question was, "Where is the praise group? Why is there only one person? Next Sunday, will the rest be there?" The preacher answered, "This is all we have; there is no more."

74

Honestly, this caused us some discouragement because where we had come from, there were some 20 participants between instrumentalists and singers.

What we didn't know was that Bro. Enrique would not leave us alone. As much as we tried to hide, he always found us. The next week, suddenly, there was a loud rapping at our front entrance, which got our attention. As I looked out the window, I saw it was Bro. Enrique, the preacher. Since my husband wasn't at home, that was my excuse for "I'm not going to open the door for him." Nevertheless, he kept on so much that I had no recourse but to open the door. And what a surprise! He had his hands full, and he was rapping so loud because he had to use his foot as he couldn't use his hands. What did he have? A huge supply of provisions for our family. He had noticed by the way we had eaten that we were in need of food. This brought great gladness to all the family as we had abundance for about a month. Also, he would give my husband some money whenever he could. We began to attend all the services of the church and to become involved in some of the ministries. We spent many long evenings with Bro. Enrique, as he astutely taught us why some doctrines we held were not in accord with the Scripture, always with much respect and love. Thus, he became our mentor, confidant, teacher, and friend, along with his wife, Sharon, and the rest of our families.

After a few years, my husband, through his responsibility and hard work, was promoted at his job; our economic state began to change, and we were able to buy a house in a subdivision quite a way from the church. But that didn't keep us from attending church, and we continued there with enthusiasm and the desire to learn daily. When the day came for us to receive the deed to our house, yes, the brother who accompanied us that day was Bro. Enrique. Our beginning there was beautiful because we were able to pray for our new home before entering it.

We continued in our work and learning and, in this way, grew daily in the knowledge of the Scriptures with much zeal and desire to know our Lord more.

After a time, one morning and with no previous symptoms, Paco fell down the doorstep at the entrance of our house and wounded his head. We hurried to the hospital, and he was hospitalized because he had some weakness in his legs. The doctor suspected a cerebral hemorrhage from the way the fall happened, as Paco said his legs had just doubled under him. After several hours, we received the diagnosis: Guillain Barre syndrome. We had no idea what that was, but the doctor explained that it is a disorder in which the immune system damages the neurons and causes muscle weakness and paralysis. There are different levels of severity with this disease, and Paco was at the highest level. In just a few hours, he became completely immobilized; he could only move his eyes. His whole body was paralyzed. This virus literally destroys muscles, including damage to internal organs, such as the stomach, intestines, lungs, heart, brain, and others. So bodily functions so simple for us, such as swallowing saliva, he could not carry out. He was hospitalized for almost a month. The doctor told us daily that it would be his last, that we should be prepared for the worst, and that we should let his family in other places know so they could be with him. His family came almost immediately. The church began a great prayer campaign for his health, and we were covered by our grand family in Christ. The virus began from the bottom and worked up, which meant the damage began in his legs and moved up. The doctor feared that if it reached his diaphragm, it would cease functioning and throw him into respiratory arrest; if it reached his heart, it would cause cardiac arrest; and what would happen if it reached his brain? Horrible news daily! There was spiritual warfare 24 hours a day. When the virus reached his diaphragm, it went around his lungs and heart and stopped just before reaching his brain. Almighty God!

Paco was released from the hospital, but his legs were quite damaged, and he was confined to a wheelchair. He had physical therapy daily for at least two hours, so we went to the hospital almost mechanically every day, rain, cold, or snow. He couldn't miss therapy for any reason. Those were three long years during which he had to battle his paralysis, but, yes, daily, we saw improvement. And we celebrated it eagerly, for he was like a baby learning how to take his first steps. Finally, he recovered almost all his functionality; he only had a few after-effects in one leg, but he could walk all right. We were delighted with this and, above all, with how God had worked in his body. This was a great testimony to other ill brethren. That was when we became even more committed to the Lord. Paco was healthy and still had his job.

Several years later, during which we put all our effort into learning more about our Lord and being disciplined by our brother Enrique, we were hit with the announcement that they would be leaving the church because they had felt the call to go to Amarillo, Texas, to work for the Lord. What? They would leave us alone in the church in Independencia #1? How could this be? What would become of us? What a catastrophe! It seemed that we would lose our beloved preacher and his family. How terrible! Suddenly, we didn't know whether to pray that they would not go, that it would not go well for them there and they would return, or that God would impede their leaving. But it didn't happen like we wanted it to.

Suddenly, the church was called to make a big decision: who would be our new preacher? The day came, and we voted with much order, respect, and prayer. Surprise! Brother Francisco Rodríguez Márquez, or Bro. Paco, as he was known affectionately, had been elected by God and by the church as the new preacher of the Church of Christ in Colonia Independence #1. Were we happy? No! We were trembling with fear; we understood perfectly the responsibility that lay ahead of us as a family. Even so, we stayed to serve the church with much fear at first but always with the help of God and under Bro. Enrique's supervision, who came at least once a month to correct the errors we committed, which were numerous. And, yes, some people left the church because they weren't in agreement with the election.

Nevertheless, we promised ourselves that we would serve the Lord with all our strength and heart in the ministry with its highs and lows, always putting the Lord in the first place. It was a lot of work because my husband was still working secularly, so our work was multiplied. We were happy, serving the Lord and being accountable to Him and Bro. Enrique each time he visited us. Unfortunately, my husband again began having problems with his health. This time, he had an inguinal hernia that caused much pain and caused his abdomen to become swollen and bother him. So, on our next visit to the doctor, he thought it strange that Paco had liquid in his abdomen, and without worrying about the hernia, they investigated why he had liquid in his abdomen. He was hospitalized, and again, we received a terrible diagnosis: cirrhosis from medicine. All that they had used in his previous illness had damaged his liver. Nevertheless, they controlled it and began to draw the liquid from his abdomen. By doing this, he became more able to function. He had no complications during the next three years, even though we noticed that he was tired almost all the time.

The time came for the camp the church organized every year, and we went there quite happily. But mid-week, he began to vomit blood, and we went to the town hospital, where they told me they didn't have the means to help him there. They recommended taking him by ambulance to Cd. Juárez, some five or six hours from where we were, hospitalizing him there and trying to stabilize him. After about four weeks of struggling, Paco died at peace, without pain, and surrounded by those he most loved: his family and brethren in Christ. Did I feel like dying too? Yes, I don't deny it. I had a lot of "whys." Where had God been? Why this since we had served Him so much . . .?

What I am going to say may seem strange, but what a great funeral! So many people loved my husband: brethren, friends from work, family, children, and grandchildren! There were so many songs praising God; what a wonderful farewell for a servant of God! But then, what would happen next?

I knew there would be changes related to the ministry in the church; Paco was no longer there, and what would happen to me? I don't deny that, after his death, the hardest thing was to leave behind much of what I did in the church, for someone else would take his place and mine. I was accustomed to a lot of activity, and to hear suddenly something like, "You, not anymore," devastated me terribly. Above all, I noticed that the reasons weren't the best; it seemed like I was "in the way." I went through a terrible desert, and even though there were many times I didn't want to go to church, I conquered the desert with God's help and didn't quit congregating with them. In spite of everything, with my heart aching due to many circumstances, I continued with what was necessary for the church to move along with God's help and with new leaders that God was raising up. That is and will always be my beloved church.

God doesn't make mistakes and always has wonderful plans that don't fail. So, a young couple began to take charge of a ministry in the city of El Paso, Texas, SAEM (Spanish-American Evangelistic Ministries). When I learned what they were doing there, I liked it a lot; inside, my desire was that I could sometimes be part of this ministry. He was the son of Bro. Enrique Meza, who had, unfortunately, died about four years after my husband's death. How sad! Then Jonathan Meza came on the scene with his wife Nadia as director of SAEM.

By this time, my family life was completely different compared to what it was while my husband was alive. My older daughter, Ana, was married to Steve Meza, and they were parents to four children, my beautiful grandchildren. My younger daughter, Rebeca, was married to Erick. They have no children (but I hope they do soon). So I could carry out my ministry peacefully since my responsibilities as the mother of single daughters had ended. The peace of knowing they are married to men of God and who serve Him is priceless. Proverbs 22:6 *Train up a child in the way he should go; even when he is old, he will not depart from it.*

During one of his visits to my home, Jonathan Meza suggested that I might enjoy helping at SAEM, and I immediately answered, "Yes!" That was what I had wanted to begin with. Here, I make a parenthesis because, even though I answered "yes" immediately, it wasn't easy to decide. I went round and round with the issue, making some excuses about accepting because I knew all it would imply my leaving: church, family, home, etc. Why do I say this? By this time, my daughter Ana had begun proceedings to apply for my residence in the United States, and this meant I couldn't cross over to my beloved Juárez for at least three to six months. I took heart and prayed a lot, attentive to God's guidance, and began to turn over my ministries: the class I had been teaching for years in the Bible Institute, the class I taught on Wednesdays in church, the praise ministry, and the preparation of the children's class in Sunday School and during church.

Some asked me, "But why are you leaving everything? How can you do this: leave family, church, your home, your belongings, your friends, and everything for which you've worked? But . . .?" I can't explain it, but I'm sure that God is going to use me in other areas. I only know that I feel good: I am at peace and sure. I'm not saying that I won't go back! Of course I will! In fact, my prayer is that the proceedings will go quickly and I can visit my family, brethren, and friends.

Now, my job in this place is to write new tracts about quite controversial themes, all based on the Scriptures and teaching only what they teach. I must say, also, that SAEM took me in with much generosity, affection, and respect, just as if I were part of the family. I'm more than thankful for that.

There is so much I could tell about, but I want to mention only what will benefit those who take the time to read this book. In my case, a beautiful Psalm helped me, and I even memorized the 1st chapter. Part of verse 3 says: *"That yields its fruit in its season."* Without a doubt, the Lord has control of my life, and He will allow me to bear fruit when the perfect time comes.

Finally, during the difficult times I've gone through, I have had the blessing of having close-by Christian women, friends, family, and my daughters, who have been present in those most difficult times in my life and have supported me so I could continue. I'm not going to mention anyone in case I should hurt someone by leaving her out, but I am infinitely grateful to each one of you who have listened to me, dried my tears, and spoken encouraging words. My petition to the Lord is that He bless you greatly until the blessings run over.

Glory and honor be to our God!

1 Timothy 1:17 *To the King of the ages, immortal, invisible, the only God, be honor and glory forever and ever. Amen.*

Chapter – 3
Rooted
by Angie Cooperider

I first thought about ministry when I was in junior high, and my minister pulled me aside and asked me the question, "Have you ever thought about being a minister's wife?"

I answered, "I would like to be a youth minister's wife, not a minister's wife." After that, I did not think much about that question, although it was still in the back of my mind and would pop to the front from time to time. Little did I know what God had in His plans for me and my future.

I am a girl raised in the South. My dad worked for the Government and was transferred quite a bit, so I don't have one place that I call home. I just consider the South my home. I grew up with great examples of Christian parents who taught me how to love the Lord. I became a Christian and was baptized when I was twelve. I enjoyed going to and working at church camp, attending youth group, Bible Bowl, and leading a Bible study when I was in junior high and high school. After high school, I attended and graduated from Milligan College. After graduating, I moved to Manassas, Virginia, to begin a career with the Bureau of Alcohol, Tobacco, and Firearms (ATF). I worked in Washington, DC, for about seven months before moving to Greensboro, North Carolina, where I continued my career as an ATF inspector from April 1989 to May 1992. During that time, I volunteered at the homeless shelter serving meals and took an active role in our women's ministry at church.

Tom was born in Rochester, New York, but primarily grew up in the North, living in Michigan. His family lived in Stevensville, Michigan, until Tom was in seventh grade. He then moved to Owosso, Michigan, where he began his eighth-grade year, graduated from high school, and was very involved in the youth group. Tom attended Central Michigan University from 1983 to 1987 and was very involved in the Christian Campus House there. He actually lived at the Christian Campus House called His house his senior year. Tom started out his college career in business and then changed to biology. He ran out of money before finishing and had to move back home. His parents had moved to Westlake, Ohio, and were attending Westlake Church of Christ.

Tom started and led a youth group while at Westlake Church of Christ. The senior minister, Tim Hanze, talked to Tom about attending

85

Bible college and going into youth ministry. Tom felt the Lord's calling to pursue youth ministry, visited several Bible colleges and decided on Johnson Bible College (now Johnson University). Tom attended Johnson from August 1989 to May 1992.

Tom and I met in December 1990 at Westlake Church of Christ on a Sunday night. I was home spending a week with my family at Christmas, and Tom was on his semester break at Johnson. We ended up sharing a hymn book that night as I had my wrist in a cast from a recent surgery. After the Sunday evening service, Tom asked if I would like to do something during the week that I was at my parents. I told him yes and to just give me a call. He called, and we had our first date on Friday, December 28, 1990. We went to see "Dances with Wolves" and then went to Friendly's Restaurant and got a Coke.

We often joked after we were married that we only got a Coke at Friendly's since they are known for their ice cream, and I love ice cream. Our dating consisted of many letters written in the mail, long-distance phone calls, and once-a-month visits alternating between Johnson Bible College and my apartment in Greensboro, North Carolina. I knew by March 1991, after only three months of dating, that Tom was the man I wanted to marry. I was not ready to say "I love you" yet, but I knew deep down that God had brought him into my life as my future husband. Tom was actually the first one to say, "I love you," and when I did not immediately say it back to him, he said it was okay. He would be patient and give me time. It only took about a month after he said those words for me to say them back to him. Tom was very genuine and kind and had a servant's heart. He loved the Lord and lived every day trying to deepen his relationship with Jesus. Tom helped deepen my relationship with Jesus as he was always learning and sharing what God was teaching him. I never had a self-esteem issue, as Tom was always encouraging me and boasting about my talents. Tom loved me big and selflessly.

Tom proposed in June 1991, and I did not hesitate to say YES. Tom and I married in May 1992; he had just graduated from Johnson Bible College and accepted a youth minister position at Windfall Christian Church in Windfall, Indiana.

We worked together in leading the youth group, but my passion was for the preschool children. Tom would lead the children's church (ages Kindergarten to 5th grade) on Sunday mornings except when the senior minister was on vacation, and then he would fill in and preach. I usually taught the two's and three's Sunday school classes. We also volunteered to work the junior high week of church camp, where we chose the wilderness weeks. The wilderness weeks took place offsite and involved canoeing, backpacking, high ropes courses, and white-water rafting.

Our first son, Jacob, was born on April 23, 1995. Tom and I were nervous and excited about becoming parents. Jacob arrived on a Sunday afternoon, and a revival at church was scheduled to start Sunday evening. Tom had prepared a children's lesson during the preaching time each night of revival. Tom's senior and junior high students were able to take his notes and teach the younger kids on Sunday night so Tom could stay at the hospital with me. I don't remember exactly how I felt or how Tom felt about the church event colliding with our family event, except Tom was so proud of his kids for stepping up and using their gifts. His heart was overwhelmed with the joy of being a father and seeing seeds planted, producing fruit in his students.

I remember the first time Tom preached at Windfall and how proud I was of him. He was not perfect and improved over time, but he preached from the heart, not wavering from what God's Word said. This was our first time to ever live in a farming community. Tom and I both grew up living in the suburbs.

Tom put considerable effort into learning about the lifestyle of those in the communities in which he served. Looking back, I can now see how important that quality was in making our ministry successful. Although he had no prior experience in farming, soon after taking the position in Windfall, he was using farm terms as if he had worked in farming all his life. Tom and I were not certain how life would be living in a small town, but it did not take long for us to adjust and fall in love with small-town life.

Everyone knew their neighbors and pitched in when there was a need. Everyone celebrated each other's victories and mourned each other's defeats. One of the foundations of Tom's ministry with men was his attendance at the Saturday morning breakfast gatherings. This became an excellent tool for Tom to learn from the men and build strong relationships with those who attended.

He officiated his first wedding at Windfall Christian Church. Our twin boys, Josiah and Jonathan, were also born while we were ministering in Windfall. When the twins were born on December 27, 1996, I left the full-time workforce to become a stay-at-home mom.

Tom's desire grew to preach more, and that led us to our second ministry. By now, we had three children, and I no longer worked outside the home. Tom began his position as senior minister at West Union Christian Church in West Union, Illinois, in March 1997.

While in West Union, Tom matured in his preaching skills and began working on his master's degree in preaching and counseling at Lincoln Christian College. He held a bachelor's degree in youth ministry and wanted to gain more knowledge and helpful tools to help him better lead people in their relationship with Jesus. Tom had a way of relating to people that made one feel welcome and important. He became involved in the community as a volunteer fireman and baseball coach. Tom and I both enjoyed serving in the community. The baseball league approached Tom each year to ask if he would coach a team, and I would volunteer at the concession stand. Some of the boys' fathers helped Tom coach, and the wives helped me in the concession stand. A special bond was formed with these baseball parents.

One of the elders and his wife took our three boys every Monday so I could run errands and grocery shop. Having three boys, two and under, made it difficult to accomplish daily chores, so I looked forward to Mondays.

I was also able to schedule doctor appointments for myself on Mondays. Mondays also provided me the opportunity to recharge so I could be the best mom possible. Tom always went over to the church early on Sundays so he could reflect on his sermon and pray for God to use him as His vessel. I was challenged to get all the kids ready on Sunday mornings alone. Another elder's wife came over every Sunday morning to help me get the kids ready for church. This was a huge act of service for me, and she and her husband became adopted grandparents to our kids. Tom loved to share the Gospel with people and really got excited when the Holy Spirit moved the individuals to make a decision and be baptized.

A fond memory I have is when Tom came home and said a lady wanted to be baptized. This was not just any lady; she was in a wheelchair, and she was deathly afraid of water. Tom, her son, and her grandsons lifted the wheelchair into the baptistry, and Tom baptized her. Tears of rejoicing and many hugs took place as we all celebrated having a new sister in Christ.

Tom also represented our church at the North American Christian Convention and gave a testimony of the giving above and beyond the tithe of a congregation made up of 150 members. He was nervous about speaking in front of thousands of people, but he was excited to share the strong faith the church in West Union demonstrated. I was nervous for him as well, but very proud to see him used by God to represent His faithfulness.

While serving in West Union, Tom and I had the opportunity to participate in a faith promise rally. Our faith was challenged as Tom filled out the faith promise pledge card and submitted it. Tom and I had talked and prayed about an amount we would give monthly. He filled out the pledge card and "accidentally" checked the weekly box. He came home and told me and said he would correct it. I told him, "No, if you checked the weekly box, then we will give our pledge amount weekly instead of monthly." Neither of us would have realized how much God would bless us and provide for us if Tom had not "accidentally" checked the wrong box. We received money in the mail one day, and it was just the amount we needed to pay a bill. A family in the church needed an air conditioning unit, and we were able to provide one anonymously to them. I was able to stay home and not work outside the home the entire time we ministered at West Union. Our faith grew and deepened during our time at West Union. God always provided for us. We were not rich monetarily, but we always had money to provide for our family and their needs. Our focus turned from ourselves to others. We both wanted to bless others the way God had blessed us. We constantly thanked God for allowing Tom to write the pledge amount in the weekly category and not the monthly category.

Tom officiated at more weddings and funerals and provided counseling. I would usually be Tom's reminder at weddings to have the guests sit down after the bride made it down the aisle. After I could not get his attention at one wedding and everyone stood the whole time, I made it a point to sit so he could see me. I did not participate much in the counseling at this time in Tom's ministry as the kids were very young and could not be left alone. I participated in the women's ministry and taught elementary Sunday school classes. I was also involved in a mom's support group through the Robinson Christian Church and attended conferences once a year. Tom and I also worked church camp together, and both sets of our parents would take turns coming to watch the kids. Our daughter, Jenna, was born on September 12, 1998, while we were living in West Union.

We both volunteered in the school system and taught an abstinence-based sex education class to 7th graders and 9th graders. We had a student from our church come up to us and tell us we reminded him of Penn and Teller since Tom did all the talking, and I wrote information on the board and passed out the papers. This made us both laugh because it was very true. I was quiet, introverted, and did a lot behind the scenes, and Tom was an extrovert, a people person, and loved leading. Tom was able to relate to people of all ages and had a way of meeting them right where they were. I did not notice this quality right away. It was only after reflecting and looking back that I realized what a gift Tom had.

Our daughter started kindergarten in August 2004, and that allowed me to accompany Tom on hospital visits, nursing homes, funeral visitations, etc. We loved doing ministry together. Tom would always greet everyone with his infectious smile, and it would light up any room. We would both talk and share stories with those we visited, but Tom would always talk and share more than I did. We ended all our visits by joining hands and praying.

During our first two ministries, we lived in the church parsonage. It helped our family by allowing me to not have to work outside the home once we started having children. The church was always accommodating in allowing us to paint and make updates when necessary. We hosted the elders and their wives over at our house on Sunday evenings when there was an elder's meeting and the board members and their wives when the board met. This allowed us all to get to know each other on a deeper level, as some of those meetings were long. This was the beginning of our hospitality ministry.

In the Fall of 2004, Tom received a phone call from a church in North Carolina asking if he would be willing to consider being their senior minister. We had to sit down and pray about that decision. One of the advantages of moving to North Carolina was that we would own our own home because the church did not have a parsonage. We would also be closer to my parents but farther from Tom's parents. It was never an easy decision to leave a church and go to another.

We had made some very dear friends, and our children had their own set of friends. We all shed tears when the time came for Tom to preach a trial sermon in Fayetteville. Our hearts were sad to leave dear friends, but we were excited about the opportunities moving to North Carolina would bring.

Tom accepted the senior minister position at Fayetteville Christian Church in March 2005. Our four children were in kindergarten, 2nd grade, and 4th grade when we moved. Tom took a salary pay cut when we moved to North Carolina, and the first year, I subbed some at the preschool, led a ladies' morning Bible study at the church, and volunteered at the elementary school the kids were attending. The preschool director position became available during our second year at Fayetteville, and I was offered the job and took it.

Tom was the face of our ministry, and I was the nuts and bolts behind it. Tom was a 100% lion personality and loved being around people. He would always talk to every person at a church event. I, on the other hand, had a beaver personality and would find a few close friends I knew and stick with them throughout the event. I loved being in the background and not having attention drawn to myself.

I had the gift of hospitality, and Tom and I hosted many families over the years in our homes. Tom would carry on the conversation throughout the visit while I would prepare and serve the meal. Throughout our ministry together, Tom would take a lead role, and I would serve as the support role and provide encouragement. We worked well together and complemented each other on our strengths and weaknesses. Tom made people feel comfortable without compromising the Gospel message.

Tom would find some common ground with whomever he was talking to and strike up a conversation. He then would find a way to share Jesus with that individual either through a personal story or experience or scripture that came to his mind that related to the conversation. He was gentle in his approach but always spoke the truth. His life's motto was helping people take one step closer to Jesus. Tom was direct and to the point in his preaching and did not waver from the truth of the Bible, no matter the subject matter.

We loved to have people over and share the gift of hospitality. While in Fayetteville, we hosted a care group at our house, and whenever former members would come back to visit, we would host a meal at our house and invite those in the congregation who knew the family over to visit with them. Tom touched a lot of lives through the church, community, and social media.

94

One comment I often heard after Tom passed away was, "I really miss his comments on Snapchat, Instagram, Twitter, and Facebook. I always looked forward to his comments each day." Tom and I responded to several family crises together while serving in the ministry. At times, it meant we had to sacrifice family times or planned events and put the needs of the church before our own. We both knew serving in ministry meant you were on call 24/7.

This took some adjustment at the beginning of our ministry and marriage. We made a point to have regular date nights and to spend days off doing something we enjoyed, which strengthened our relationship as a couple.

On occasion, when a church crisis occurred on our planned date night or day off, we were able to adjust and just reschedule our time at a later date. While in Fayetteville, I oversaw funeral dinners and meals for people having surgery, welcoming a baby, or losing a loved one.

The ministry in Fayetteville was very different than our first two ministries. It was predominantly a military town and congregation. Fayetteville was the home of Fort Bragg, and Tom was soon using acronyms in conversations with soldiers. He quickly established himself as a student of military life and learned all that he could to better understand the military community. Military families were impressed that Tom would take the time to understand their life and language. The military spouses were especially grateful to Tom for making sure their loved ones were taken care of and their needs met while they were deployed.

After Tom's passing, many shared stories of him, some of which I did not even know. Hearing these stories showed the character of who Tom was and how he was perceived by others and brought joy knowing others recognized the love he and I had for doing ministry together. Our very dear friends we met in Fayetteville are the Smith family. The Smith family came to Fayetteville in 2008, and Kevin remembers the first time he met Tom. "I remember walking into the side door next to the office, where I encountered Tom, Lyle, and Damien. They were all very welcoming and eager to answer my questions and quick to provide tips on where to go and not go in the greater Fayetteville area. The thing that stood out to me most about Tom was how genuinely sincere he was as we were talking about our families, FCC, and sports. I knew right away this was my kind of guy." Shortly after the Smith family arrived, Kevin deployed for a year. During deployments, Tom and I made it a point to help families stay connected. One Valentine's Day, Tom helped Kevin arrange a singing quartet to perform for his wife while she was teaching at the church preschool. Tom set up a video chat so Kevin could witness the event. I partnered with a mutual friend to bless Kevin's wife each month of the deployment and count down to his return. Tom was able to help another deployed soldier connect to his wife when he was unexpectedly sent to a conference in Florida. Tom called me and told me Casey was going to be stateside for a week, and we needed to get Debra down to see him. I brought Debra to Tom's office, and he found a plane ticket with a military discount and booked the trip. He took Debra to the airport. I went and stayed at the couple's house and took care of the kids and got them to and from school. On another occasion, Tom was able to help this same family out by checking their teenage son out of school early to see the Star Wars movie. Tom and I were the hands and feet for these families to utilize and help them stay connected while being so far away. We both loved seeing the smiles and excitement it brought to the spouses and children when these surprises took place. Our friendships with these families grew deeper through each deployment. This is just one area where Tom showed himself as a true servant leader. We knew God had placed our family in Fayetteville at this time to minister, in particular, to military families that pass through.

Kevin had numerous church-related encounters with Tom and the other church leaders. "We never had a dull meeting. Like clockwork, we always had at least one issue or topic that would lead to spirited discussion. Tom always had a knack for bringing the discussion back into focus so we could make a decision and move on to the next matter of business. I appreciated that quality about Tom. He let the other leaders feel empowered to work through issues, never trying to dominate a meeting or steer it in any one direction; he trusted his leadership team to make the right decision."

Families not only felt that Tom was a huge supporter of the military but saw it in action. Any opportunity he had to thank someone in uniform, and he did. When you live a military lifestyle, you often find yourself far from family, and when special events happen, it is sometimes difficult to have family present for promotions or other special events. Tom was included in several military retirement parties, promotions, and graduation ceremonies. Kevin fondly remembers Tom and a mutual friend driving hours to attend a 30-minute graduation ceremony. Tom also provided the prayer at Kevin's promotion to Lieutenant Colonel and drove multiple states to support Kevin during his Battalion Change of Command and again to his promotion to Colonel.

Who Am I Now That He Is Not Here?

Our families share many wonderful memories, and we all miss Tom. We know Tom was glad to see his Father even though our hearts felt it was too soon.

Tom had a lasting impact on many people and invested in many lives. I am grateful for the friendships Tom and I have made in the ministry.

The church in Fayetteville consisted of 30% native North Carolinians and 70% of transplants. The turnover was very high due to the military moving families. The church had a new face about every three years, which meant we were saying goodbye to friends quite often. A piece of our hearts was broken each time a close family moved away. It meant we had to find new Sunday school teachers, nursery workers, elders, deacons, and worship leaders. It was frustrating at times to fill in the gaps people left in the various ministries of the church. We learned to try new ideas and ways of doing ministry and not rely on the old traditional ways that had worked in the past. I was more emotional outwardly when close friends left, and Tom had to console me on many occasions. He handled the goodbyes easier than I did; however, after thirteen and a half years, his heart could not take it anymore. He started to become callous when new families would visit FCC and think to himself, "Why bother? They will leave in three years anyway." He knew that thought process was not good for him or the church, but he also knew I loved my job and living in the South. He even briefly considered getting out of the ministry so we could stay in Fayetteville. I told him immediately that he had a special gift as a minister and he did not need to leave the ministry. I told him that as much as I loved my job, I loved him more and would follow him wherever he found a church. It was a very difficult decision to make because we left very good friends behind, but both of us felt the Holy Spirit leading us throughout the process.

We both believed that it was apparent that we would move and serve at another church if we were going to remain effective in ministry.

Tom applied for the senior minister position at Solsberry Christian Church in Solsberry, Indiana, in March 2018. He selected this church because it would get us closer to his parents, who were aging. He preached a trial sermon in May 2018 and accepted the senior minister position at Solsberry Christian Church. We moved to Solsberry, Indiana, in August 2018 and lived in the parsonage.

This move was a big adjustment for me and caused me to step out of my comfort zone. After directing the preschool in Fayetteville for 12 1/2 years, I left the education field and returned to working for the Government.

This meant I was working full-time again when, in the past 23 ½ years, I had worked at home or part-time. I was apprehensive about going back to work full-time at a job that was unfamiliar to me. However, the Lord had his hand over this situation and knew I needed to be in this job at this time. The job provided good medical insurance, retirement, and a guaranteed salary, which God knew the kids and I would need. Tom and I were both glad that I would be working for the Government again and dreamed about the retirement it would provide for us.

Tom loved visiting people and finding out how life was going for them. We would be riding around town, and if someone from the church was out mowing, he would stop and say hello. Tom was very good at sitting with people while loved ones faced surgery and checking on people in nursing homes and hospitals. Tom also loved attending sporting events and supporting the kids in the congregation. Tom was very good at relating to people no matter what their age.

Tom was a present husband and Father. He was all about what was important to us and made a point of encouraging the kids and me to do what we enjoyed. He attended the kids' sporting events, orchestra concerts, and banquets and made it a priority to be in attendance when it was possible. People knew they were important and mattered both in the church, outside the church, and in our family.

We both wanted to buy a home and move out of the parsonage once we sold our house in Fayetteville. God also orchestrated this process. We purchased our home in March 2019and moved out of the parsonage into our home in April 2019. It was only eight months later that our life changed forever with the unexpected passing of Tom.

Tom preached his last sermon on December 29, 2019. He was experiencing a sore throat, which we attributed to just a cold, and so he did not shake hands with anyone after church that Sunday. Our family left after church and headed to Ohio to spend a week with Tom's parents.

On Monday, Tom's throat was still bothering him, so we thought it might be strep throat. I asked him if he wanted to go to urgent care, but he declined. Tuesday morning, we woke up and ate breakfast. We were deciding what we were going to do for the day because Tom's dad was having a dental procedure, so we knew we would not see them. Tom was his jovial self. We decided to go to the art museum in downtown Cleveland. By this time, it was early afternoon, so Tom was napping while the kids and I were still deciding on what to do. Once we decided, I woke him up to ask if he wanted to go with us, but he said he would stay back and rest. The kids and I headed to the art museum and then ate at a restaurant in downtown Cleveland.

Tom texted me while we were at the restaurant eating to ask when we would be home. I told him about thirty minutes as we were finishing eating, and I paid the bill. He said he wanted me to take him to urgent care when I got back. Urgent care was closed, so I took him to the emergency room of the nearest hospital to us. He walked in with me and answered the triage nurses' questions. His voice was scratchy, and I could tell his throat hurt, but he was not exhibiting any signs of breathing trouble. The nurse took us to a room, and the doctor came in to check Tom and tried to look down his throat but commented his tonsils were too swollen.

The doctor felt his tonsils on his neck and then had me feel them and asked, "Do they normally feel like this?" I said, "no". They started Tom on a breathing treatment and asked if he had eaten anything out of his normal routine. He said, "No." Shortly after, I had to call the doctor back into the room because Tom started having trouble breathing. I had to do this multiple times, and the last time, they said they would need to intubate him. I stepped out of the room, and they took me to another room to wait. It seemed like forever, but finally, the doctor came in to tell me that Tom had coded, and they got him back, and they needed to lifeline him down to University Hospital in downtown Cleveland. I had to go back to the house and tell the kids, and then I drove down to the hospital.

Tom was in the hospital for three days, but he never regained consciousness. The doctor said that his brain was dead. He was an organ donor, so they kept him on the machines in order to harvest his organs. When the doctor sat us down and told us his brain was dead, one of my children shouted, "We did not come on vacation to lose a dad." I said, "I know we did not, but we need to trust God as he sees the big picture, and we can only see what is right in front of us." I held tight to Psalm 139:16, ". . . *all the days ordained for me were written in your book before one of them came to be."*

The people at Solsberry Christian church were very supportive during my grief journey. They brought food, air mattresses, extra chairs, and a camper, as all of my family and Tom's family lived out of state. I received a lot of hugs and encouragement during this time. Some people did not know what to say to me, and others would ask, "Are you still staying in Solsberry?" I never took any comments personally. Being in the ministry for 27 ½ years helped me in extending grace to people as I recognized they were not intentionally saying or doing the wrong thing. I knew the people meant well, and their heart was in the right place.

I struggled with my purpose and my role after Tom passed away. I had been a minister's wife for our entire marriage of 27 ½ years, and I loved it. I loved helping Tom help others in their walk with Jesus. I enjoyed helping him provide advice to couples on marriage and parenting. I loved being Tom's helpmate both in our marriage and in his ministry. I found myself wondering what my purpose was and how/where I would serve. As Tom's wife, I knew my purpose and direction.

Tom was the best husband and a great example of a spiritual leader in our home. Early in our marriage, we had to learn to give each other grace and extend forgiveness as two imperfect people now are building a life together. We knew that marriage took each of us to give 100%.

We learned to divide and conquer and work together to complement each other's strengths and weaknesses. We chose not to yell when we had a disagreement but to walk away, calm down, and come back and discuss once we were not in the heat of the moment. We did not have a perfect marriage, but we had a great marriage. We loved spending time with each other and celebrating special occasions. We were married 27 ½ years before Tom passed away, and so for our 28th wedding anniversary, I decided to continue our tradition. I purchased the anniversary gift for the 28th wedding anniversary, which happened to be orchids. I got the orchids in the form of a picture and hung it above our bed. Our anniversary is the hardest day for me, but I choose to reflect on the great memories we made together.

I also struggled with staying at Solsberry Christian Church once the new minister and his wife arrived. I did not want to be a hindrance to their ministry by continuing to worship and serve at the church. I wrestled back and forth and had a lot of talks with God. After many prayers, I felt the Holy Spirit's presence with me and a peace about staying. I also consulted a good friend about my situation and explained that I did not want to be in the way of the new minister and his wife serving at Solsberry. After the reassurance from my friend and the peace I had after praying, I decided I was not hindering the ministry at Solsberry Christian Church.

I have remained at Solsberry Christian Church, as difficult as it has been. The congregation and leadership have been very gracious and kind. I knew as a pastor's wife, a search committee would need to be formed and a new minister hired. The chairman of the search committee and the elders kept me informed of the progress and let me know ahead of time when they would be making an announcement to the congregation. I shed a lot of tears through this process, and it was hard to think of someone else in the pulpit preaching, but I knew deep down that God would place the right person in Solsberry. God prepared my heart and allowed me to accept the new minister and his wife. It is still difficult and strange at times because the new minister's name is Tom. Whenever his name is spoken at church, there is a little twinge because it would have been in the same context as my Tom. I am still part of the women's ministry planning team, serve in the nursery, and teach preschool. It has been difficult not knowing the inside scoop of everything going on. Tom was very good at keeping me informed, and I now have to rely on checking emails to stay informed of what is happening. Early on, members expected that I would know all the answers, and I had to come to terms with the fact that I was not the minister's wife anymore.

Some Scriptures that have helped me through the grief journey are the following:

2 Corinthians 1:3-4 – *Blessed be the God and Father of our Lord Jesus Christ, the Father of mercies and God of all comfort, who comforts us in all our affliction so that we will be able to comfort those who are in any affliction with the comfort with which we ourselves are comforted by God.*

Psalm 23:4 – *Even though I walk through the valley of the shadow of death,*

I fear no evil, for You are with me; Your rod and Your staff comfort me.

Psalm 34:18 – ***The Lord is near to the brokenhearted***
And saves those who are crushed in spirit.

Isaiah 41:10 – ***Do not fear, for I am with you;***
Do not be afraid, for I am your God.
I will strengthen you, I will also help you,
I will also uphold you with My righteous right hand.

Philippians 4:13 – *I can do all things through Him who strengthens me.*

Hebrews 13:14 – *For here we do not have a lasting city, but we are seeking* the city *which is to come.*

Revelation 14:13 – *And I heard a voice from heaven, saying, "Write: 'Blessed are the dead who die in the Lord from now on!'" "Yes," says the Spirit, "so that they may rest from their labors, for their deeds follow with them."*

It was difficult at first to attend a care group as the only single person or go out to eat with couples, but over time, it has gotten easier.

I am more attentive to widows' needs and have been able to minister to a recent widow at our church. One of my desires is to oversee a widow's ministry. I have started by creating a widows' checklist that can be completed when one loses her spouse and then followed up by someone on a monthly basis. I believe the loneliness of widowhood is a real need that needs to be met by the church. This was an overwhelmingly common response in a poll I took among my widow friends. If money were no object, another big dream ministry would be to host a bed and breakfast for ministers and their families at minimal cost as a getaway for them to renew and recharge.

I've also dealt with the difficulty of asking for help. I am not opposed to accepting help or asking for help, but when I ask for help now, it is a reminder that Tom is gone. If he were still here, I would not need to be asking for help. It has been a process for me. It takes time for me to gather up the initiative to ask for help and then prepare myself for making the phone call.

I try to stay busy to combat loneliness. I continue to quilt as my nieces and nephews continue to graduate from high school, and I present them with a twin-size quilt.

I played church softball, which kept me active and filled up some time. I continued to visit our friends, which was difficult at first because Tom had always gone with me. I adjusted to visiting them by myself, and each visit gets easier. They have remained faithful and don't treat me any differently without Tom being around. They are willing to talk about Tom and share memories and not avoid the subject. I find it encouraging and comforting to hear stories and memories they have of Tom.

Our family dynamics have changed since Tom's death. He was very good at keeping in touch with family members by phone calls, texts, and social media. I am not nearly as good at keeping up and checking in on everyone. I do try to touch base with family at least once a week, but I am not always diligent about that. I've learned to juggle working full-time and taking care of the home inside and outside. I have a much deeper respect for single parents now.

While friends try to understand and offer comfort, you really don't get it until you have lost a spouse. Other widows get what you are feeling. You wish no one has to face the grief journey of losing a spouse, but there is some camaraderie amongst widows. I have very close friends I can share and cry with, and they are there for me anytime, but none has lost her spouse, and I hope Jesus returns before they have to experience this kind of loss. The grief journey is just that, a journey, and I am taking it one minute at a time.

Jill's August Story by Jill Giallanza

Every August 14th, what is on my mind (Facebook is always asking that question) to some degree is Evan, the years we had together, our wonderful kids, and so many, many blessings we had. Forty-one years ago, Evan and I got married. Eleven years ago, on our last anniversary, we bought this bird cage in Cloudcroft, New Mexico. I liked it.

I did not know what I would do with it, but I liked it, and he bought it for me.

After Evan moved to heaven, I put some of the flowers from his service in the birdcage and added a bird inside and one outside. I later added new colorful flowers with green leaves (fake ones).

It reminds me that this world is not all there is and that although there are times of grief, and even in those times.

God is near and is good and kind and gracious.

Beauty and joy surround me.

Last week, I caught a glimpse of that beauty. I happened to catch the sun shining through the window right on and through the birdcage. The light had a golden hue to it, casting a shadow of the birdcage on the wall. This little birdhouse reminds me that Evan is free of the sorrows of this world and is rejoicing in His presence, and it reminds me of who God is and what His plans for me are.

5 "LORD, you are my portion and my cup of blessing; you hold my future.
6 The boundary lines have fallen for me in pleasant places; indeed, I have a beautiful inheritance.
7 I will bless the LORD who counsels me - even at night when my thoughts trouble me.
8 I always let the LORD guide me. Because he is at my right hand, I will not be shaken.
9 Therefore, my heart is glad, and my whole being rejoices; my body also rests securely.
10 For you will not abandon me to Sheol; you will not allow your faithful one to see decay.
11 You reveal the path of life to me; in your presence is abundant joy; at your right hand are eternal pleasures." Psalm 16

I loved this little reminder that He is with me! "The boundary lines have fallen for me in pleasant places; indeed, I have a beautiful inheritance."

August 2023

Just One More Time by Sara Ray

I have been in a reflective mood since the month of October began. It hasn't hit me as hard this year as in the past ten years, but the dread of facing October 15th still lingers and probably will for the rest of my life. Now it is over, and I can go on again without reliving the day in 2012 when my husband Bob graduated to Heaven.

I hear so many people say that they would give anything to have just one more day with a loved one who has passed away. I have come to realize that I can't say that because being with Bob for one more day would never be enough. I would always want more. And more. And more. Although it is hard to make this statement, I have learned to be thankful for the thirty-six years, four months, and sixteen days that I had with my husband and let go of the deep craving to have more time with him. That is one wish that could never come true in this life.

I am reminded of a day with my granddaughter Vivian that happened nine months after Bob was gone. She was staying at my house for a couple of days. As we walked out to get the mail one afternoon, Vivian, who was two and one-half years old at the time, remarked that Jesus and Did Dad were in Heaven. I agreed that they were. Her next question: "Can we walk there to see them?" I informed her that we could not and that if we could get there, we would not want to come back.

Up until 2012, October has been my favorite month. After that year, I dreaded its coming because it meant I was one year further away from the time I had with Bob. Now, it seems like he was here just yesterday and forever ago. I will always miss him, but I can't dwell in the past; it is uninhabitable.

A lot has happened since the Lord welcomed Bob to Paradise. Three more grandchildren. I learned to deal with things that he would have taken care of. I have had to learn who I am all over again since much of my identity revolved around being Bob's wife. Making decisions without his input started out with the thoughts of, "What would Bob do?" I finally realized that I could choose things that he would not because he was no longer in the picture. It was done with lots of tears, but I am able to look at things more from a single perspective. And I can put all the black pepper I want in my food without feeling guilty. He is not here to care.

There is a lot that I love about October. Brilliant fall colors. Warm days and cool nights. The garden work is done. Much of the allergy-causing pollen has disappeared. Crunching through fall leaves. Ripe apples. My firstborn son arrived towards the end of the month (saving me from going to a costume party dressed as the great pumpkin). His firstborn child (Vivian) was born on the first day of October. It has been a gradual process, but I am blessed to appreciate the month again, even if it does bring hard-to-face memories.

Through the whole process of reclaiming the joy I find in the month of October, the Lord has been my Rock. He has given me strength I didn't know I was capable of possessing. He has provided people to come alongside me and help me in so many ways. He has given me a heart to help others through their own grief journeys.

Several months after Bob was gone, I asked God, "What do I do now?" I sensed His answer, "Be an encourager." And that is what I have tried to do. There are times that I have failed miserably. There are times that I have been too caught up either in my own grief or with things I think I should get accomplished to take the time to reach out to others. However, I

113

can't dwell on my mistakes, or I will become discouraged, and that goes against what I am supposed to do.

This is one of those times when I sense that God has given me a writing assignment. I am sharing it in hopes that there may be those who need its message.

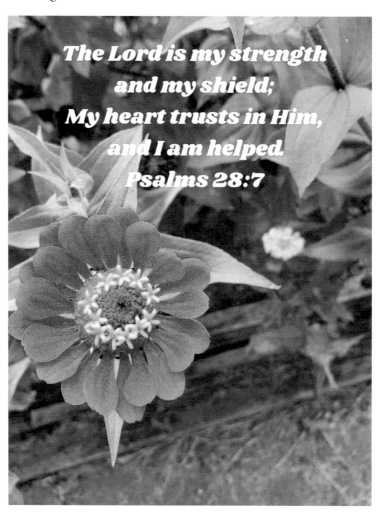

The Lord is my strength
and my shield;
My heart trusts in Him,
and I am helped.
Psalms 28:7

∞

Chapter – 4
Two Suitcases and a Plane Ticket
by Lisa Renz Choe

G rowing up in Oregon, I always wanted to be a missionary. My family always went to listen to missionaries speak in churches or summer camps. I read many books about missionaries, from Jonathan Goforth of China to Elizabeth Elliot's books about the missionaries who gave their lives for Christ in Ecuador.

From the time I was eight years old, I always picked beans in the summer to buy my school clothes for the next year. When I was about ten, my mother and my aunt arranged with the owner of one of the bean fields for us (my mother and me, and my aunt and her daughter) to stay in the bean camp for the summer. This was one room in a long building of rooms, side by side, where the transients could stay while they worked for the farmers. We worked picking beans during the day, and in the evenings, my mother and aunt arranged to have Bible studies with any of the transient families who wanted to come join us. Once, on a Sunday, the farmer loaned us the bean bus, which they used to pick up the local workers, and we filled it with our transient neighbors who had been studying the Bible with us. We drove to the nearest church, a little Holiness church with about 20 members. They doubled their attendance that day! My inspiration to become a missionary came also from my mother and aunt.

When I was 16, the Rodney Northrup family came to our church to speak, and Rodney invited anyone who wanted to come down for a six-week summer internship to visit them at their ranch in Saltillo in northern Mexico. There were about 16 young people that summer; three of us were still in high school, while the rest were in college.

That was the summer that I met Buck Renz, one of the college students. At first, we just talked a lot, and then he started taking walks with me up the hills surrounding the ranch. He would take his hymnbook and sing me hymns out of it because he loved hymns and classical music. Since he could not stay on key, I had no idea how some of those hymns went until I heard them later. One of his favorites was "Be Thou My Vision," which later became a favorite of mine (after I heard how the tune really went).

There was no electricity on the ranch, so we learned to iron our clothes with a sad iron (a heavy metal iron that we heated up on the stove), and we had to wash our clothes by hand on the scrub board.

That summer was the first time I got stung by a scorpion. I was stung in bed, and we saw it by lamp light. One of the girls had a book about desert animals, so we read all the symptoms of scorpion stings, and as soon as she would read a symptom, I immediately believed that I had that symptom. I thought I needed to go to the doctor, but there was no one to take me. Rodney had taken all the boys out to the ranches to preach and did not get back until 3 a.m. Once he returned, I informed him that I wanted to go to the doctor, but he eyed me over and said, "How long ago were you stung?" I responded, "About 3 hours ago." Rodney asked, "And do you feel your throat closing up, or are you vomiting?" I answered, "No, not really." Rodney said, "Well, I can take you to a doctor if you want, but most Mexicans would just go back to bed." So, I went back to bed, feeling creepy crawlies all night, but I survived.

Also, that summer, Rodney took us swimming at a public pool in Arteaga. I used to drink a lot of water from the pool when I swam, so I got dysentery. I had the runs so bad that the girls finally took a bucket to my room, which I sat on about every 15 minutes for three days. After three days, I went blind from being so dehydrated. The missionaries just gave me bottles and bottles of Kaopectate with paregoric, and I eventually recovered, but not before losing 12 pounds in three days.

That summer changed my life. I gave all my clothes away to a girl who lived on the ranch and had two dresses; she wore one and washed the other one. She was also missing a leg, so she walked everywhere with a crutch. I began to see how rich I really was. I met my future husband, and I became much bolder when speaking, as I now was speaking from my own experiences.

Juaquin (Buck) Renz was an amazing man. He was born in Boise, Idaho, on December 23, 1939, the youngest of three children. His dad was a carpenter, but the family moved almost constantly from place to place, wherever his dad could get work. The rest of the family worked in the fields, picking fruit from California to Oregon, to Washington, back to Idaho, and then making that trip again. Buck told me that once he made a list of all the schools that he had gone to between first and sixth grade, it came to 26. He said that some of those schools he visited more than once in their transient life.

Eventually, after he started high school, his parents settled down in Idaho, and he graduated from Caldwell High School in 1959. Buck always had a dream of becoming a pilot, so when he was in high school, he joined CAP (Civil Air Patrol). While he was in the CAP, he won a scholarship to travel to England, where he met Prince Phillip at Buckingham Palace. Buck was the first one of his family to go to college, and he started at Northwest Christian College in Eugene, Oregon. He always had to work in college, and his jobs varied from serving as a mimeograph repair man to working in the sawmills to janitor work. He loved classical music and started renting a room from the music teacher, Dudley Carson, along with several other students.

His music teacher loved flowers and natural plants and would collect wild mushrooms and fern sprouts, with which he and the young men would experiment.

One time, Buck came into the house and saw that Dudley had a bunch of mushrooms on the counter. Buck thought that he would cook them up but decided to wait because perhaps Dudley had some special use for them. When Dudley came in, he saw the mushrooms, and he announced to all the young men, "I picked these to show you the deadliest kind; you must never, ever eat these." The rule of thumb with mushrooms is to only pick those that you absolutely know are edible.

Buck said that another time, Dudley bought a fresh pineapple at the store, and since they really did not know about pineapples, it was green. Nobody wanted to eat it, but Buck decided to eat it so it would not go to waste. Buck said it burned his lips and tongue so badly that he could not eat for a week! He never liked fresh pineapple after that, and it had to be so ripe that it was almost fermented before he would eat it.

Buck and I began dating the year following our summer in Mexico. He was in his Senior year at Northwest Christian College (NCC), and I was in my Senior year of High School.

During the year that Buck and I were dating, there was a hurricane-like storm in Oregon. We were sent home from school early, so that meant I was in the house alone. The wind whistled through every crack in the walls, and the roof was shaking. I called my girlfriend, Heather, and she was crying because she was afraid the big evergreens around her house were going to fall. One did but did not do much damage to her house. Then I called Buck, and he was really worried about me, so he said he would come and sit the storm out with me. He rode his bicycle over to my house!

He said that he had to pedal down the last steep hill because the wind was that strong against him. With all the branches and tarpaper flying all around, it is amazing that he did not get hit by something during his wild ride.

When I graduated from High School, and Buck graduated from Northwest Christian College in 1963, Buck asked me to be his wife. So, I was engaged for the first two years of college. He left for Mexico the next year to work with the Northrups in Saltillo while I started college at Northwest Christian College.

I lived at home in Eugene and sometimes rode my bike to college and other times took the bus. I would get letters quite frequently from Buck.

I think I only saw Buck about three times during the next two years, and one of those times was the summer I was able to spend in Saltillo. While I was there, I bought my wedding dress. It was a beautiful lace dress that cost about $60 in Mexico, much less than it would have cost in the States. The day that I bought the dress, I went to have my hair cut, and the lady who cut my hair talked with me the whole time. I told her that I was very hot (it was a scorching hot day), but what I said in Spanish was, "*Estoy caliente,*" which means I'm hot in a sexual way. I remembered that I should not say it that way, so I said, "*Estoy muy embarazada,*" wanting to say that I was very embarrassed, but in Spanish, that means "I am pregnant." I am sure she "understood" my hurry to get a wedding dress!

During those two years that we were apart, Buck also came down with hepatitis. He was living on the ranch at that time, which is about seven kilometers outside the city of Saltillo. He kept getting sicker and sicker and finally walked into Saltillo to find a doctor. After the doctor examined him, he left the room for a very long time. Buck thought that the doctor had forgotten about him and just did not think he was that sick, so he got off the examination table and walked back out to the ranch.

A few days later, he was really sick and asked a fellow worker to drive him back to the doctor, where Buck said he was going to insist that he was sick and try to convince the doctor of that fact.

The fellow worker, Lowell Tate, said that his own grandfather, the day before he died, looked better than Buck that day. When he walked into the doctor's office, the doctor exclaimed, "Where have you been?"

Buck said, "I came back because I really think I am sick." The doctor said, "I left the room to call the hospital to get you a bed, and when I came back, you were gone!" So, the doctor put him in the hospital immediately for the next three days. Buck said that during his stay, one of the nurses could not find a vein, so the lady who was mopping the floor took the needle and found the vein. He said this was back when they used glass syringes and reusable needles and just sterilized them over and over. Since the doctor had emphasized to the nurse to never use his needle on anyone else, she thought she was supposed to use the same needle on him. So, one time, when the nurse came in to give him a shot, he asked her to either find a hammer to put it in with or to go buy another needle, and he gave her the money with which to do that.

When he got out of the hospital, he still had to have shots but did not have anyone to give them to him, so he gave them to himself. He said the first time, he grabbed the skin, stuck the needle in, and it went right through and poked him in the finger, so he had to do it again! When he got back to the States, his doctor friend in Idaho sent him to have some tests and said that his results, six months after he was sick with hepatitis, were still so high that the doctor did not know how he had survived!

I spent my sophomore year of college traveling with my friend, Gail Zilkowski, to churches all over Oregon, Washington, and Idaho, singing and showing slides of our summers in Mexico. She had worked in Aguascalientes, and I had been in Saltillo. Our theme was, "Here am I, Lord; send me."

Buck and I were married in 1965. Buck had saved up all the money that he had earned during the two years that he was in Mexico, and we were able to make a down payment on a brand-new red Volkswagen Bug, which cost us a total of $2,500. We had a car payment of about $30 a month, and our apartment near the college cost us $65 a month. We received a donation from his church, the Caldwell First Christian church in Idaho, $150 a month, so we both worked that first summer of our marriage. He worked two jobs, one in a sawmill and the other repairing office machines, and I worked ten-hour nights in the cannery. I think the only time we saw one another was from 5 a.m., when I got home from work, to 6 a.m., when he left for work in the sawmill. However, we were able to pay our school bills.

Buck began school at the University of Oregon, and I was a junior at Northwest Christian College. He began to study a Master's program in International Studies, but he decided to go over to the Journalism School because his vision was to improve the Christian literature that he had seen in Mexico. While he was making this decision, he consulted with some former professors at NCC, and one bluntly told him that he was not a good enough student to make it at the U of O Journalism school because it was one of the top ten schools in the USA. He left that meeting and talked with the dean of the Journalism school about his dream of improving the books and pamphlets that he had seen in Mexico. The dean suggested that he only take the Journalism classes that he would need to get another undergraduate degree, which is what he did. Due to his motivation, he did very well in the Journalism School.

Our last year of school was quite challenging. During the summer, my mom had some surgery on her legs, and she needed to be near us for care. She had been living near Portland, and we needed to transport her down to Eugene. Our little Volkswagen Bug was too small, so we borrowed a station wagon from some friends. On the way down from Portland, the engine blew up, so we spent that summer working to pay for that engine. Northwest Christian College had given us a job as house parents in one of the dorms so my mom could live with us for the summer. When school time came, we had to move her into an apartment across the street and pay the rent. Both Buck and I worked all the next year to pay for both my mom's and our own food. On weekends, we drove to a little church in Deadwood, Oregon, near the coast. Buck served as a minister, and I served as a Sunday School teacher.

We spent the following year traveling around the Northwest, raising money to go to the mission field. In the summer of 1968, we went to Cuernavaca, Morelos, a city of about 600,000 people south of Mexico City. We spent the next 40 years in Morelos, creating Christian literature, publishing a magazine called *El Discípulo Cristiano*, and helping to establish several churches in Morelos. Our four children were all born in Cuernavaca: the twins Raul and Roberto (whom we called Robi) in 1968, Rafael (Rafi) in 1972, and Tabitha (Tabi) in 1985. At first, we lived in two houses in Bugambilias, a colony of little cement houses. We used one house for the office, and we lived in the other one.

Many things happened to us while we lived in Bugambilias. One time, we came back from the States with a whole bunch of dented cans that someone had given us. They did not have labels, so we never knew what we were going to eat when we opened a can. Shortly after we came back, a whole busload of 28 people visited us, and they arrived right at lunchtime. I started opening cans, and we made an enormous soup that fed everyone just fine.

The twins got into anything and everything. We had a picture of Robi when he was about two, climbing up the narrow shelves that Buck made to go behind the kitchen door. When they were about that age, they ate at least five Christmas tree balls off the Christmas tree. I know that it was at least five because there were at least five different colors of glass in their mouths. All the doctor told me was to give them bananas and soft bread to eat to help the glass go through.

The next Christmas, we did not have any money for Christmas presents. Buck made each one a toy with a block of wood, drilling holes in it and putting screws in each of the holes. That and a screwdriver were their Christmas toys that year, and they loved it! Buck said it was the best Christmas present he had ever given them until the kitchen door fell off its hinges; they had taken out all the screws.

One day, we found Robi with an empty bottle of children's aspirin in his hand. We were not sure if only Robi had swallowed the aspirin or if he had "shared" it with his twin brother, Raul. At that time, Dr. Glenn Hancock lived with us, and he figured out a way to pump out both the twins' stomachs with a plastic tube and a suction gun. So, they both got their stomachs pumped, but only Robi had the aspirin in his stomach.

We were frequent visitors to either doctors or the emergency room of the hospital. Among drinking kerosene, a bottle of worm medicine, eating a slightly poisonous plant called Elephant's Ear, and putting a tangerine seed up a nose, we kept the doctors busy. One week, we had the back of Raul's head sewn up and Robi's forehead sewn up.

Dr. Glen knew about Robi's accident but not Raul's, so when we asked Dr. Glenn to take out Raul's stitches, he looked at him and stated, "It's a miracle! He doesn't even have a scar!" he looked at his forehead. We turned Raul's head around and said, "No, this is the other one."

One day, when we were in Bugambilias, I spent all day at the Satellite church helping with the Vacation Bible School. When I got home, I prepared a paste of flour, water, and a little sugar to be used for making piñatas the next day. I was tired and went to bed early, leaving the pot on the stove. Later that night, Buck came home with a young man from Mexico

City, whom he put to sleep on the couch in the living room. When I got up in the morning, I went to get the paste to take to the church, and about half of it was gone. I asked Buck if he knew anything about it. "Oh, that was paste?" he asked. "When we got home last night, the young man was hungry, and we saw that pot on the stove and thought it was mashed potatoes!" I ran over to see if the boy was still alive! Buck said, "We ate it and thought it tasted a little strange, but it was filling."

The Satellite church was meeting in a tar-paper shack when we started going there. The men of the church would go out to the state of Guerrero twice a month to visit men in the prison in Teloloapan, a village about three hours away in the mountains. Many times, Buck would drive them out there and back, and they always stopped at a large market in Iguala for breakfast. One day, the men bet Buck that he could not eat anything spicier than they could as they walked past the bins of about 15 different kinds of chiles. Buck accepted the challenge with this condition: "I get to choose the spicy food." They looked over the chiles and decided there was not anything there that they could not bite and chew down, so they agreed. He went directly to the onion bin, picked up a big white onion, took a bite out of it, and offered it to the next man.

"But that's not a chile!" they protested. "I didn't say 'chile,' I said, 'spicy food.' Onions are hot, are they not?" They all had to agree that onions were hot, and Buck won the bet after about three bites.

One year, the Satellite church put on a Christmas drama of "The Fourth Wiseman." Buck was the fourth Wiseman, and at the end of the story, he collapsed and "died." The twins (who were about four at that time) ran up to him from the audience and cried, "Papi, Papi, are you all right?" That made Buck laugh, so there he was, "dead," shaking like a leaf. Everyone in the audience laughed, too; it made for a not-so-dramatic ending to the play.

Christmas day changed for our family after we started going to Satellite. It had always been a family day when we opened presents and had a large Christmas dinner. It was baptism day for Satellite when they went to the river and baptized everyone who had recently become Christians. Everyone took a picnic lunch, and we made it a church family day. At first, I was a little put out that we had lost our traditional Christmas day, but after thinking about it, there can be no better way to celebrate Christmas than to add new members to the body of Christ!

I read a book, The Passover Plot, that started all kinds of doubts in my mind as to whether God really existed or not or if He were just something we made up to satisfy the desires of our heart. I still taught Sunday school but felt like a hypocrite because I had so many doubts. One day, when we were still living in Bugambilias, I was in the bathroom, and the twins and Leti (a little girl we had taken in from the orphanage in Mexico City) were running around the house. I suddenly heard a door slam and someone wailing like a banshee. I quickly exited the bathroom, running into the kitchen, where Leti was shaking and pointing to the steel kitchen door. I opened the door, and there on the hinge side stood five-year-old Robi with his finger smashed into a hamburger there in the door. I picked him up, ran to the bathroom, wrapped the finger in toilet paper, and ran out of the house to a doctor's house about three blocks away.

The doctor was not there, so I shouted for Buck to get the keys to the *combi* (Volkswagen bus) so we could go find a doctor. I held Robi on my lap all the way to the doctor's office, which was clear on the south end of town. About halfway there, Robi forgot about his finger and started pointing to the houses on the way, saying, "*Casa, casa, casa . . .*" ("House, house, house . . ."). I started looking at the houses, and the thought came to my mind, "I don't believe that those houses made themselves. I believe there was an architect, or at least a designer, and a builder who placed one brick on another. The bricks did not just do that on their own. If I believe that such a simple thing as a house did not build itself, how can I believe that the body of this, my child, just somehow made itself out of the primeval slime? Look at his little finger, so intricate, so delicate, all smashed like that." That was the beginning of my journey back to faith; ever since I have told people that it is all right to have doubts about your faith because doubts make you have to reason out why you believe what you do.

When we got to the doctor's office, he had a whole yard full of patients waiting for him. However, when he saw us, he rushed us into his office and took Robi out of my arms. That is when I fainted. Robi received seven stitches in his tiny finger. The doctor bandaged him up and instructed me to change the bandage in three days. The next day, I found Robi with his bandaged hand in the toilet, so we went to the doctor to get another bandage. When I told the doctor what had happened, he said, "Hmmm, vitamin Pee, well, there are worse things." "I don't want to know about them," I declared. Somehow, Robi's finger survived, but he still has a scar on that finger.

We moved out to a squatter colony when the twins were ten and Rafi was six. We lived for nine months without electricity and nine years without running water. I remember counting the scorpions that I found in the house that first year; when I got to 200, I quit counting. I think we all got stung at some point during that first year, so I always had antihistamines on hand. When the neighbors learned we had them, they would come to our house when they got stung. At first, we all lived in the one room we had constructed, and we continued to build the rest of the house room by room. Since I was an only child, and she had nowhere else to go, my mother also came to live with us when she retired from teaching. When she moved in, we had added a kitchen, a bathroom, and another bedroom, so it became her room.

We began a small church in that neighborhood. The leaders of the group who started the colony gave us two lots, one for the church and one for our house. Our ministry in the church was in addition to the literature ministry, so for a while, Buck was the minister of the church and also preached in another five churches located around the area. We gave seminars for couples both in the church and in home groups when our children reached marriageable age.

While we lived in Pro-Hogar, Tabi was born when I was 40, the twins were 18, and Rafi was 13. When Tabi was about ten months old, she began to vomit everything. I took her to doctor after doctor. They checked her for allergies to milk, and one doctor ordered X-rays of her whole digestive system. The doctor said that Tabi's stomach was exceptionally large and that the barium that went to the stomach should empty in about 5 minutes to the small intestine. But in her case, the barium stayed in her stomach for more than 45 minutes and only drop by drop entered the small intestine. The x-ray revealed a blockage that required surgery to repair.

However, the doctor stated that she was too small due to not being able to eat.

During this time, the church in Pro-Hogar surrounded us with love. I was in a sea of tears at that time because I thought my daughter was going to die. One Sunday, the minister stood up and announced that the whole church was going to fast and pray the next day. I thought, "Lord, I've never fasted in my life." Then I thought, "How will I make it without my morning coffee?" Finally, I thought, "How am I going to let my Mexican brothers and sisters fast and I not? Anyway, Tabi is basically fasting every day." So, we all fasted the next day. The next Sunday, I was still crying, so the minister announced, "Our sister is still grieving for Tabi, so we are going to fast all the next week." I almost gasped, "Lord, I already fasted one day! How can I do it for a whole week?" But then he announced, "We are going to fast each day until 3 p.m." I thought, "Ah, okay, I can do that." Meantime, Buck had gone to the States to find us a house to live in during the next year of furlough in Eugene, Oregon. When I told him about fasting, he fasted for the next three weeks.

Tabi began to get better; I thought God had healed her, so I took her to have X-rays again, and they came out the same! So now we had two sets of X-rays a month apart that showed the same results. We continued to consult with doctors along our way to Oregon (we had various doctor friends in Colorado, Idaho, and Oregon). A total of seven doctors all agreed that she needed surgery. However, she kept improving all along and wound up never having surgery. I did not want to tempt God with another series of X-rays, but we simply praised Him for the miracle!

Buck was diagnosed with cancer in 1992 when he was visiting his sister in Idaho who had cancer. I took Tabi with me to Idaho while he went through the first treatments, and then we went back to Mexico for more treatments until about 1997. Then, a doctor friend invited us to go to Alabama for more treatment. We were there until it was obvious that there was no more that could be done for him. We returned to Mexico, where my mother was bedridden from having had one of her legs amputated. In the first few months of 1998, I was taking care of both my husband and my mother. When my husband died in August of 1998, I was still taking care of my mother. My sons were all married and no longer lived at home, but my daughter was 13 when her father died.

After my husband died, the church in Idaho that supported us said that since he was the missionary, they would only support me for the next ten months, and then I would have to figure out what I was going to do. My home church in Oregon had died, so there was no hope of support from there. I had a few friends who supported me, but I knew it was not enough to live on. I thought it would be impossible to take my Mom back to the States unless I hired an ambulance to take her, and even then, I had nowhere to go. So, I just began to pray for God's guidance. I thought I might be able to continue publishing the magazine if we could get enough support and my sons could help me with the layout and design.

Not long afterward, my forwarding agent called me to tell me that my home church had sold its building and divided up the money among the various missionaries that they had supported. My portion was twenty-five thousand dollars. So, I took that as a "yes" and decided to continue publishing the magazine until I ran out of money. My mother died three years after my husband died on my daughter's 16th birthday. I continued publishing the magazine until my son, Raul, went to the USA, and then I had no one to do the layout and design.

In 2003, I drove my daughter up to college (Johnson Bible College in Knoxville, Tenn.) and then drove all the way back home by myself in my little Nissan two-door sedan. Then, as I was alone, I married a Mexican man whom I met through his daughter. He was almost 20 years older than I was. We were married for only five years, but during that time, we opened a perfume shop, and I learned to make perfumes. We also sold cream to clean mechanics' hands, as well as a secret recipe for *adobo* (dry rub) for chickens, which we sold to people who sold rotisserie chickens. When he died five years later, also of cancer, I decided that I wanted to find some area of Christian ministry.

I began communicating with a man (Dr. Victor Vaca) in Ecuador who had set up a foundation to make microloans for women's groups. These loans helped them set up small business ventures or buy farm animals to sell. He invited me to come to Ecuador to see how they worked. I told him that I did not want to go as a tourist but that I was willing to teach some workshops, so he set me up with three workshops in one week. I taught one group to make *adobo*, another to make the cream for cleaning hands, and the third group was a seven-hour workshop on Christian education. From there, I went to Chile for two weeks to be with my daughter, who is a missionary there, and then back to Mexico. I did not hear from Dr. Vaca in Ecuador for about a month, so I thought perhaps he had not liked my workshops. But after about a month, he wrote to say that he had been very sick in the hospital and that he had three groups coming down in the summer to do mission work. He needed me as a translator. I told him I had to sell my hand cream business and find someone to live in my house, but that I would go. That is how I ended up in Ecuador. I packed two suitcases with clothes, bought my plane ticket, and I was off to my next adventure!

I ended up staying in Ecuador for six years, doing all kinds of things. What I did most was drive the pickup all over the Andes mountains to take the workers in FEDICE (Fundación Ecuménica para el Desarrollo Integral, Capacitación y Educación, *Ecumenical Foundation for Integral Development, Training, and Education*) to their various workshops. Occasionally, I also did a workshop on making perfumes, making unbaked cookies (a lot of the women do not have ovens), preparing *nopales* (prickly pear cactus leaves, which they have but do not eat), how to make the cream and adobo, and the last workshop I gave was on baking a cake at 13,000 feet!

We also did Vacation Bible Schools and other projects in the churches. Usually, though, I was tired after driving for two to six hours, so I rested while my companions gave workshops on using computers and making new food dishes with native plants, such as quinoa or beans. Another of the workers was a zoo technician, so he taught the women how to castrate their animals, how to give them vitamins and vaccines, how to buy better breeds so that they had better production, how to make use of earthworms for fertilizer, etc. I loved my time in Ecuador. Even though Dr. Vaca died after I had only been there about six months, I stayed on to help everyone else with the foundation.

While in Ecuador, I was beginning to have problems seeing at night, and I was forced to do a lot of night driving as we returned from the villages (the sun comes up at 6 a.m. every morning and sets at 6 p.m. every evening in Ecuador because it is right on the equator). Every so often, I was getting on a site called Christian Café, which matches up people who are singles. One day, I saw a new man who said he was looking for a missionary, so I sent him a wink and told him to look at my profile and, if he was interested, we would talk. That is how I met my third husband, Frank Choe, who came to Ecuador to propose to me after we had been writing to one another for about six months. He has a Christian non-profit organization that is directed at doing research to find ways to reach people of other faiths, such as Muslims, Hindus, Buddhists, and people who follow Confucius' teachings.

It is called Cotari, and you can see what he does at www.Cotari.org. Right now, he is writing a book on reaching Muslims with their highest authority, the Koran, and he has given several seminars on the same topic. He gave me some papers to proofread, and when I saw what they were about, I decided to read the Koran, which I had never read before. So, I read it in a couple of months, giving him my opinion on some of what I had read. He says that is what convinced him to marry me – because no one that he had taught the seminar to before had ever read the Koran all the way through! So, I packed my two suitcases and bought my plane ticket, and here I am, in California, with a whole new direction in ministry. I guess God is not finished with me yet. The Scripture that has been my theme along this journey is Habakkuk 3:17-19:

Even if the fig tree does not blossom,
And there is no fruit on the vines,
If the yield of the olive fails,
And the fields produce no food,
Even if the flock disappears from the fold,

And there are no cattle in the stalls,
Yet I will triumph in the Lord,
I will rejoice in the God of my salvation.
The Lord God is my strength,
And He has made my feet like deer's feet,
And has me walk on my high places.

Chapter – 5
My Story
by Ana María Herrera

A rturo Herrera Flores was born in Nueva Rosita, Coahuila, Mexico, on March 9, 1949. At the age of 15, he emigrated to the United States with his family, where he and his parents and siblings worked until he was 21. Arturo and his brothers, Ricardo, Feliciano, Antonio, and Pedro, began attending the Buena Vista church in Piedras Negras, Coahuila.

Who Am I Now That He Is Not Here?

I, Ana María González Flores, was born in Piedras Negras, Coahuila on April 28, 1952. My parents were Manuel González and Sara Guerrero. I am the youngest of their children. Thanks to God, I was born into a Christian home, and from childhood, very young, at five years old, I began singing in church. Later, at 15 years of age, I taught toddlers and primary children in Sunday School at the Colonia Buena Vista Church of Christ in Piedras Negras. I was always active in the church, leading songs and participating in dramas with the youth in May and December. I really enjoyed attending camps and national youth conventions and the local ones held monthly in Piedras Negras, my birth city.

Arturo and I met in the Col. Buena Vista church. I was just 15 years old, and he was 18. However, Arturo told people that he knew me before then, that he had seen me standing at a store window downtown and said to himself, "I'm going to marry her!" When he began to court me, I didn't immediately respond positively. But with time, we began a formal relationship of four years, accepted by both our families, and were married in the Buena Vista church in April of 1971. And we began, rather continued, our activities in that church.

Afterward, in need of better-paid work, we decided to move to Chicago, where we had family living. We lived there for almost four years, attending the Blue Island Christian Church, where Bro. Sergio Alvarado ministered. The climate in Chicago was very cold! After an especially cold winter, we decided to move to Texas and lived in east Dallas for over a year. Later, we moved to San Antonio (many moves in a few years, but, without a doubt, God was accommodating things for the beginning of our ministry and service to the King).

We were living in San Antonio and attending the Bellaire Christian Church, where Bro. Dámaso García was preaching. As Arturo took a more active part in the church, teaching Sunday School classes and helping with

140

the youth, the Lord laid it on his heart to prepare for the ministry in an institute. So, Arturo decided to enter Colegio Bíblico in Eagle Pass, TX. We talked and prayed about what this decision would entail. Arturo had some business to take care of before we could move. Also, we already had our four children: Arturo (11 ½), Isaac (10), Elías (six), and Hananí, our only daughter (about five). I gave him unconditional support but with one "little" warning, "If you begin, you must finish without any excuse!" Why did I say that? We knew that many students abandoned their studies without finishing them.

We moved back to Eagle Pass, TX, in 1982. The first year was quite difficult. Why? We had four children and lived on the college campus, so our economy was quite poor. We worked on campus for our food and lodging (we ate what was served in the dining room) and could visit our parents and eat with them at times. But there was no spare money. For Arturo, it was more difficult because he had to study for middle school and college classes at the same time. He had only studied primary school (grades one through six) and a technical secretarial course. So, he had to make double the effort to succeed. He was 34 years old, and the majority of his fellow students were youth who had finished high school, and some had even studied at the college level. However, I was always there to support him.

When my mother began taking adult education and sewing classes (she had only had two years of schooling) in Piedras Negras that year, I provided transportation for her. I took our little Hananí with me and took advantage of the time to take classes in cosmetology and cooking. Our sons stayed with the other Colegio Bíblico children.

After our first year at Colegio, we went that summer with a group from Colegio to work in the city of Mérida, Yucatán, in Mexico. We lived for a month with the Calderón family: Bro. Apolinar and Sis. Susan and their children. They treated us like family. We were quite happy there in a beautiful city with an excellent family. We worked in some villages nearby, and I remember one called Xocchel. We had services in the evenings with a good attendance of the brethren and a lot of children, which the girls and I took charge of. Those were unforgettable days. The Word of God touched many hearts, and quite a few people were baptized; I don't remember exactly how many. I remember that several of them were baptized in a *cenote* (deep, natural sinkhole). I also remember that we held services at the Calderón home outside at night. What a wonderful God we serve!

The whole time we spent there, Bro. Polo and Sis. Susan treated us wonderfully even with a full house – our group leader (Bro. Juan Mauricio, a Colegio Bíblico graduate and minister), a lot of students, Arturo, our two youngest children (Eliás and Hananí), and I. Bro. Polo, always so kind, took us to the churches, different places, and to the homes of families where we visited. We helped in the evangelistic campaigns, VBSs, visits, and home Bible studies. Arturo also helped preach, and I helped prepare meals. I remember that the brethren in one church there, I think it was Xocchel, cried and told us, "Don't go; don't go! Don't leave us! Stay here!" And I remember that one of the young people, a girl named Marina, later entered Colegio Bíblico. We learned of her decision when we saw her there, and this gave us great joy! What beautiful memories! We were working together with great contentment, and our children were very happy, but the time had come for us to return and for my husband to continue his studies at Colegio Bíblico. Arturo had just finished his first year of studies, and we had our goal: he could not give up his studies.

The next three years in college were less difficult economically. Arturo was given a paid job at school, and I, with the help of the wife of another student, was able to get food stamps that helped us buy food, especially for our children. We and other married student couples became older siblings for the younger students, and many of them would visit with us in our homes. At that time, it wasn't customary for student wives to study at the college except for an occasional course. I took part in the school choir during this time, and we continued helping in the Buena Vista church in Piedras Negras. Thanks to God and much hard work, Arturo was able to graduate from Colegio Bíblico in 1986 with excellent grades and received a scholarship to study at Cincinnati Christian Seminary.

I remember when we went to Cincinnati, we struggled greatly with English, especially I because among the six of us, I knew the least English. I don't know how (I know through Whom), but I understood the classes and preaching in English. Arturo studied for two years in the seminary, always struggling with the language and also working to support us. We went on Sunday mornings with one of his professors to a church in Kentucky and in the evenings to the church in Bridgetown, Ohio.

Our brethren in Cincinnati encouraged us to begin a Hispanic church in Dallas, TX, so we arrived in the northern area of Dallas at Valley View Christian Church. Arturo began meetings in Spanish there, and later, we moved them to Dallas Christian College. Later on, we moved to another place. We were there for about three years. I worked in a dental clinic while Arturo worked cleaning buildings.

Then came the opportunity to begin a church in Carrollton, TX. We bought a house there, and Arturo began working cleaning buildings to support us. He found a church building that was closed and was able to buy it. Actually, it was in a neighborhood of economic two-bedroom houses, and they adapted it by tearing down the wall between bedrooms to make more meeting space. After that, we needed more space, and a lot was bought with God's help. This time, without consulting me, Arturo mortgaged our house to buy it. I only remember that he took me to the bank, where a man was waiting with some papers that Arturo had signed and asked me to sign. When I asked what they were, they told me, and I agreed and signed. It took four years for us to build the church building because the brethren worked on it as they could. Arturo challenged the families to give $1,000 each as they were able to in order to carry out the construction. We lost five families who did not agree with the plan, but the rest remained faithful there. The women of the church made tamales to help raise money and went to the nearby town of Collinsville to sell them. The church there received us well and even began helping in the construction and encouragement. We still have a wonderful fellowship with that congregation. Also, brethren from the Bellaire church in San Antonio helped in the construction. Arturo served as minister in Carrolton for 25 years until the Lord called him into His presence.

My husband had begun having health problems years before, having been diagnosed with diabetes when he graduated from Colegio Bíblico, but he never wanted to follow a regimen of treatment and control. Because of this, he began having kidney problems that resulted in his having hemodialysis treatments three times a week, which brought on complications. Our doctor recommended a kidney transplant. The immediate option was for one of our children to donate a kidney, but neither he nor I agreed with this as we considered them too young to do so. But Arturo's condition worsened. So, with much prayer, we all had analyses and tests to see who was compatible with my husband, and even though all of us were compatible, one son and I were the most compatible. So, I gave my husband a kidney! We had the operations in 2003, and they told Arturo the kidney could last him some 16 years with proper care. But he didn't follow through, and several years later, the kidney failed. Again, he had to go through hemodialysis treatments. Then, he was responsible for cleaning a huge gymnasium, and I helped him. Our children did at times, also. As time went on, Arturo could no longer drive, so I would take him to the hospital for his hemodialysis, go to work, hurry home to clean up, and go to pick him up. He would be exhausted after each treatment. Later, he had an accident and injured a toe but didn't go to the doctor or care for it. It became infected, and by the time he went to a specialist, it was too late to save the toe. So, he had to have it amputated. Then, he had three light strokes, the last of which left him barely able to swallow food. Even so, he worked at it and became able to eat again. Oh yes, he always enjoyed eating, especially with other people! Also, his vision became more and more impaired until he could hardly see. Even though he had to quit his job, he never stopped preaching, visiting, and taking an active part in the church. Our children were grown by then and helped as they could, but they had their own lives and responsibilities.

During this time, I became affected by the stress and began having panic attacks. When I had one, I felt I couldn't breathe, and I was unable to speak. I still had to continue helping Arturo, working, and helping at church, but I was embarrassed to do so because I never knew when I would have an attack. One time, I was driving home from picking up Arturo when I felt my arms and legs drawing up. I told Arturo I was going to take him home and then go to the hospital, but he insisted that I go straight to the Emergency Room. There, they examined me, made the diagnosis, and prescribed medication. Thanks be to the Lord, in a short time I was feeling well again because life hadn't stopped being hard with all that was going on with Arturo.

At the end of his life, Arturo spent more and more time in the hospital. He died there on March 15, 2010, at 61 years of age. It was a devastating time for me. I had been left without my spouse, my children, without their father, and the church, without her minister. I had no income because I had left my job to care for Arturo and didn't qualify for my part of his disability benefits. I had to sell the house where we lived and had only about $1,000 left after paying off the mortgage. I also had to sell our car. So, I was left with nothing; I had lost my husband, house, transportation, and work in the blink of an eye. But God didn't abandon me. About nine months later, I took a job at JC Penney, where I worked for almost ten years until that branch closed. Thanks to God, they transferred me almost immediately to another branch, where I worked for another year and a half. I retired in April of 2022 at 70 years of age after 11 years with the company. I had begun receiving the widow's benefits from Arturo's disability pay during this time. I was able to buy a small mobile home, where I now live, and pay for where it is located. Even though the rent goes up yearly, until now, I've been able to get ahead in life with God's help.

I never really asked myself what my heart's desire was about God before my marriage and about what God would want for my marriage. Maybe it was because I married at a relatively young age. But even so, it never entered my mind to stray from the way of the Lord in my life. I have served the Lord since I was a young girl of 14 or 15 and taught the children in Sunday School. I have always enjoyed doing that, and I did for many years in our ministry when Arturo was at Colegio Bíblico and when we began the work of the Lord in Dallas and San Antonio. We enjoyed much support from God and the churches in Collinsville and San Antonio, who helped us lay the foundation and build in Carrollton. My desire for the Lord has been the same since Arturo decided to serve Him. I always supported my husband in the ministry because he served the Lord with all his heart; he loved His work and never considered that in this way, we would become rich, financially speaking. He always wanted to do God's will, serving Him out of love for Him, and the work, and the brethren in Christ. And I, too, wanted to keep on doing His will, serving Him daily in what I could in His church, both inside and outside.

Since Arturo died, I have never stopped serving the Lord and will not. I am sure of this. I have always supported the Lord's work as I have been able to teach children and young people, leading singing, etc. Thanks be to my Lord and God for His care in my life! He has never abandoned me! And this was even in spite of a situation that arose when a sister and I, one Sunday morning, arrived at the same time at church. I was about to enter, and she was getting out of her car and spoke to me, "Sister Ana María, there you are as forsaken as ever!" That was her greeting, and I don't deny that it affected me; it made me very sad, but I knew Whom I trusted. I don't know why she would say such a thing to me; I only greeted her and went into the church. But I don't think she was right; I was not without help. Now, we greet each other and work together in the church. I don't know why she said that to me, but God has taken all those hurt feelings I had away. God in no way ever abandoned me; He is with me! Yes, I have had difficult times, but I know that He always cared for me, even though the first two or three years after Arturo's death were really hard for me.

I thank God that our children now have families and jobs and are faithful to our Lord. I have 11 lovely grandchildren and one great-grandchild now. I have always been able to count on the support and love of the family God has left me with.

On one occasion, when Bro. Jair and Sis. Norma Castillo spoke at our church; they invited me to accompany them on their missionary trip to Cancún, Quintana Roo, Mexico. I was elated with their invitation because I always wanted to do such things, but I had to have permission from my job. Thanks be to God, they gave it to me, and I was able to go. There, I helped prepare meals and serve them, taught children's classes, led singing, helped interpret for some sisters who only spoke English, and helped the children understand what they wanted to say to them. I was only able to go on that occasion; well, one has to cover expenses, and I was still working at that time and didn't have good economic solvency. Since I was alone, it was more difficult for me. Even so, in spite of that, I thoroughly enjoyed that trip, working for the Lord! Even now, I continue to be and will always be faithful in the way of the Lord and hope to serve Him until He calls me home.

I believe it's now a little late for me, but I would have liked to have been a missionary full-time. It is a beautiful ministry because we serve our brethren with much love, and the Lord gives us the strength to do so. May He work His will in my life!

Just a few months ago, I was in Colorado as a missionary, helping some of Arturo's family who are advanced in age and need assistance. I spent almost a month there. My family missed me and asked when I would return. And there in Colorado, they were quite sad because I had to go back to my family. I also had my church responsibilities. So, in this way, it wasn't easy, on the one hand, wanting to stay but at the same time having to return to my family and church.

I really enjoy these types of activities. I carry them out very joyfully because I do so for the Lord. Now that I'm retired, and as always, the Lord supplies my economic needs, I don't have to ask anyone to provide for my expenses. That makes me feel really good because I do it for the Lord! To Him be the glory!

I don't deny that I miss my life companion and still feel his lack in my life. But God has been my good and faithful Companion and Lord, to Whom I go with any need because He dries my tears. He is my Sustainer, my Counselor, my Helper who does not fail, and He listens with love without judging, reproaching, or criticizing me; He is always there when I need Him! Glory be to Him!

Here are some of the Scriptures I loved (and still love) when we were working for the Lord and at Colegio Bíblico back when we were young:

Psalm 1 – *Blessed is the person who does not walk in the counsel of the wicked,*
Nor stand in the path of sinners,
Nor sit in the seat of scoffers!

² But his delight is in the Law of the LORD,
And on His Law he meditates day and night.
³ He will be like a tree planted by streams of water,
Which yields its fruit in its season,
And its leaf does not wither;
And in whatever he does, he prospers.
⁴ The wicked are not so,
But they are like chaff which the wind blows away.
⁵ Therefore the wicked will not stand in the judgment,
Nor sinners in the assembly of the righteous.
⁶ For the LORD knows the way of the righteous,
But the way of the wicked will perish.

Psalm 23 – *The LORD is my shepherd,*
I will not be in need.
² He lets me lie down in green pastures;
He leads me beside quiet waters.
³ He restores my soul;
He guides me in the paths of righteousness
For the sake of His name.
⁴ Even though I walk through the ʲvalley of the shadow of death,
I fear no evil, for You are with me;
Your rod and Your staff, they comfort me.
⁵ You prepare a table before me in the presence of my enemies;
You have anointed my head with oil;
My cup overflows.
⁶ Certainly goodness and faithfulness will follow me all the days of my life,
And my dwelling will be in the house of the LORD forever.

Psalm 100 – *Shout joyfully to the LORD, all the earth.*
² Serve the LORD with jubilation;
Come before Him with rejoicing.
³ Know that the LORD Himself is God;
It is He who has made us, and not we ourselves;
We are His people and the sheep of His pasture.
⁴ Enter His gates with thanksgiving,
And His courtyards with praise.
Give thanks to Him, bless His name.
⁵ For the LORD is good;
His mercy is everlasting
And His faithfulness is to all generations.

1 Timothy 4:12 – *Let no one look down on your youthfulness, but rather in speech, conduct, love, faith, and purity, show yourself an example of those who believe.*

1 John 4:8 – *The one who does not love does not know God, because God is love.*

Now that I am alone since Arturo went home to the Lord, I still love the Scriptures. Especially these verses (among many others) have really helped me:

Matthew 28:20 – . . . *"teaching them to follow all that I commanded you; and behold, I am with you always, to the end of the age."*

Psalm 39:7 – *"And now, Lord, for what do I wait? My hope is in You."*

Joshua 1:9 – *"Have I not commanded you? Be strong and courageous! Do not be terrified nor dismayed, for the LORD your God is with you wherever you go."*

Psalm 17:8 – *Keep me as the apple of your eye; Hide me in the shadow of Your wings.*

Psalm 22:10-11 – *I was cast upon You from birth;*
You have been my God from my mother's womb.
Do not be far from me, for trouble is near;
For there is no one to help.

Psalm 25:21 – *Let integrity and uprightness protect me, For I wait for You.*

Psalm 27:5 – *For on the day of trouble He will conceal me in His tabernacle;*
He will hide me in the secret place of His tent;
He will lift me up on a rock.

My prayer to the Lord is that what I Have written will be to edify and bless you who have taken time to read this book. May God bless you abundantly!

Chapter – 6
God Opened the Doors
by Susan Ogden Calderón

S ome people grow up knowing what God wants them to do. As I grew up in a Christian home in Knoxville, Tennessee, I had exposure to visiting evangelists and missionaries from a young age and knew by the time I became a Christian at ten years of age that God wanted me to become a missionary nurse — to Africa. So, I graduated from nursing school at UT Knoxville in 1964 and from Johnson Bible College (now

Johnson University) in 1967. I had recruit status from the African Christian Mission and my support, and I only lacked my passport to go to the mission field when I went to my first National Missionary Convention (now International Conference on Missions – ICOM) in Dodge City, Kansas. As I entered the convention center with the couple I had ridden with, we ran into a missionary couple they knew, Larry and Garnet Cuyler, who were serving in a rural area of northeastern Mexico. When they learned I was a nurse headed for Africa, they exclaimed, "You can't go there; you need to come and help us!" They explained that where they served, no medical help was available within around a 60-mile radius; they did what they could with their mostly common-sense knowledge and a little medicine taken in from the United States. I agreed to pray about their invitation during the convention and to give them an answer before it ended. God opened the door to Mexico, and I went through and never looked back.

I arrived in Sandia Chico, Nuevo León, México, with the Cuyler family on Thanksgiving Day, 1967, and worked with them as a nurse and in Bible teaching, youth work, and church-planting until the beginning of 1969. This ranch in México is in an arid, high mountain plain dotted with small villages (*ranchos*). At that time, the whole area had no electricity or running water, and much was reachable only by oxcart tracks or dry arroyo beds (we were some twelve miles from the nearest highway). Drivers had to become experts in mounting the center ridge and one or the other side of the tracks.

Most of my medical work was carried out consulting under a huge, ancient cedar tree next to where the missionaries lived (at first, they lived in a large tent with a small trailer for their kitchen; later, they built a large adobe house). With God as the Doctor, I delivered over 40 babies, with one stillborn (the second-born of twins, double breech with the cord wrapped between her legs and around her neck) and one born with severe cardio-respiratory problems who lived only several hours. Unfortunately, we

155

couldn't care for him or get him to any hospital before he died. I attended the births by *quinqués* (kerosene lamps), flashlights, or candles in the small house trailer converted to a "clinic," later in a clinic built into the Cuylers' house, and occasionally, in village homes for over a year. Also, I set some broken bones and sutured some wounds, along with giving hygiene and dietary instructions and dispensing medicine. After I gave preliminary aid, we transported a girl bitten by a rattlesnake to a clinic in Matehuala, San Luis Potosí (about 60 miles) for treatment with anti-venom. God saved her life. Part of the time, one of the local teenage girls helped me after I trained her to take histories and vital signs. I came back briefly to the United States in early January 1969 and then went to *Casa Hogar para Niños* (a children's home) in San Luis Potosí, San Luis Potosí, in February to fill in for several months as a girls' housemother, working with Ted and Wanda Murray. I returned at the end of June to Sandia Chico for their area VBS programs and, in mid-July, traveled to Knoxville, TN, to prepare for my wedding. Now, I take a step back to clarify that.

Shortly after arriving in Sandia Chico, I met Apolinar Calderón Arias from the neighboring *rancho* of La Trinidad through the medical program. After he became a Christian in March 1968, he expressed a desire to preach the Gospel. God opened the door, and he entered Colegio Bíblico (Bible College) in Eagle Pass, Texas, that fall. The next spring, we saw God's provision to marry and did so on August 16, 1969, in Knoxville. I returned to Eagle Pass with him to a job for which God had opened the door as Director of Nursing Service at the Maverick County Hospital District. During our five years there, we served the church in the Colonia Bravo in Piedras Negras, Coahuila, México (right across the U.S./Mexico border). Our experiences there provided great help for our life in Yucatán. At Colegio Bíblico, I served as the school nurse and taught a class I had developed, *Salud y Cuidado en el Hogar* (Health and Care in the Home), from 1970-1974. Our three children (David – 1970, Elizabeth – Lisa or "Liky" – 1972, and Marcos – 1974) were born in Eagle Pass.

While in Eagle Pass, we sought God's guidance as to where He wanted us to serve in Mexico. We wanted to go somewhere where there was no Christian church (we wanted to follow Paul's plan in Romans 15:20, *"And in this way, I aspired to preach the gospel, not where Christ was already known by name so that I would not build on another person's foundation"*). We planned to engage in church planting and leadership training. God opened the door for us to go to the Yucatán Peninsula. After Polo's graduation in June 1974, his investigative trip to Yucatán to check on local housing and living costs, and Marcos' birth, we traveled to Knoxville about mid-August to raise support. When Hurricane Fifi devastated Honduras that fall, IDES Inc. (International Disaster and Emergency Services) asked us to be Field Agents to make an investigatory trip to Honduras to assess for their recovery aid. So, Marcos, Polo, and I went in December and spent several days in San Pedro Sula, La Lima, and Progreso, visiting government agencies and NGO shelters (especially the Red Cross) and taking pictures to document damages. That experience served us for later work with IDES in Yucatán with other hurricanes.

We arrived on the field in Mérida, Yucatán, in June of 1975. (Can you imagine our family of five, a young man, and my sister-in-law all traveling in a VW Fastback from Eagle Pass, Texas, to Mérida with our clothing, a few toys and other items, and David's Big Wheel tied on top?) Once in Yucatán, we joined Professor Herb Watkins and a group of students who had just arrived from Colegio Bíblico in Eagle Pass, Texas, staying in the home of Samuel and Betty González. We immediately began helping with a week of VBS and evangelistic services in Huhí, a village about 44 mi. from Mérida. (Samuel, a Colegio Bíblico graduate, and Betty had arrived in Yucatán as missionaries in 1973 and had a small group meeting in their home in Mérida and had a contact in Huhí at the time we arrived.) As a result of that week's efforts, 11 people were baptized into Christ. That was the first congregation we saw established in Yucatán.

Here, I make a digression as to our settling in in Yucatán. We lived in rental housing until God opened the door for us to buy our own property. The second rental had a windmill for water, but it never worked right. Praise God, our neighbor across the street allowed us to get water from their yard spigot.

We moved into our own home in the Colonia Roma in April of 1976. It consisted of two concrete-block rooms (13 ft. x 16.4 ft.) and a "shack out back." We had electricity, and our water came from a backyard well, which was half ours and half the next-door neighbor's (oh, I didn't mention that the two rooms shared their walls with the neighbor's two rooms). Polo eventually built a false wall between our living room and theirs to mute noises from one side to the other (especially squeaky hammock hooks at night). A full bookshelf in the other room solved the problem there. Our street was one block from "the end of the world," the last street open at the time in that area of town, and was a narrow dirt road that ran into a two-lane dirt road, which led to the main highway of Mérida. The roads were filled with holes, which made for lots of puddles for the neighborhood children to play in during the frequent rains.

As soon as we moved into our home, Polo began building a bedroom and a bathroom. He had been a construction foreman in Monterrey for a while before I met him. Over time, he built another bedroom and kitchen downstairs and built two bedrooms, each with its bathroom, and a laundry room upstairs as well. We eventually had city water and telephone service added to our neighborhood, as well as had our street paved. The city has expanded so that now our house sits in an urban area with two shopping plazas and a Walmart a few blocks west.

Our house soon became the neighborhood gathering place for our children's friends, and we never knew how many we'd have at our table for lunch or supper. The neighbor children learned that we didn't allow foul language or bad behavior, and "regulars" quickly taught newcomers the "ground rules."

I added a plug here for missionary children: they definitely form part of the mission. Without "evangelizing," as we usually think of that activity, our children influenced their friends. All three of our children were active in the churches, beginning by helping serve Communion and taking up offerings and later helping in Bible School, VBS, and youth activities, and David would preach at times. They saw a number of their neighbor friends come to Christ as they grew up. Even some families came to Christ through their own children's influence.

After helping to begin the church in Huhí, we worked with *Hermano* (Brother) Benito, a former Presbyterian *obrero* (worker) from there, and the González family to begin congregations in Zavala and Sotuta beyond Huhí by the end of 1975. Through a Bible correspondence course contact, we received from Bro. Bill Hoff, serving in Querétaro, Querétaro, Polo met a family in the village of Xocchel, which is on the way to Huhí. God opened the door to begin Bible studies in their home, resulting in a number of baptisms in the summer of 1976 and the beginning of a congregation there.

Aside from caring for our children, as well as whoever else was around, and tending to household chores, I prepared Bible school lessons with some type of student activity each week for worship services and taught the children (babes-in-arms up to mid-teens) during the preaching time. Some of our supporters had given me some flannelgraph lessons, which I used and adapted as I could, making the characters and scenery multi-purpose. When I had construction paper available, I prepared activities with it, but mostly, I traced or drew pictures to color and made copies of them using two sheets of carbon paper. Each week, I prepared from 50 to 100 activities.

In June of 1975, I contracted Hepatitis A. I gave our family gamma globulin injections and prayed for their health, and none of them contracted the disease. God is good! Once I was well enough to travel, we went to the *rancho* for me to continue recovery, made a trip to Eagle Pass to see my doctor there, and returned to Mérida before school started.

After our return, Bro. Samuel continued the work in Huhí, Zavala, and Sotuta while we continued in Xocchel and began holding Bible studies and Sunday worship services in our home. One of the brethren in Xocchel donated a lot for a *templo* (church building), and Polo helped design and build it (he did so for three more later on in Mérida). We also began a church in northern Mérida in early 1976, which later dissolved and became two other congregations in Mérida in the early 1980s. We saw a third congregation established in Mérida a few years later and one in another village in the latter 1980s. Thanks to God's work in the hearts of the men with whom Polo worked in leadership training, a good number of them learned to teach and preach and helped lead in the congregations where they served.

Polo and I dedicated ourselves to home and church Bible studies, visitation in the areas around the congregations, youth work (both), preaching and leadership training (Polo), playing the keyboard for services, weddings, and *quinceañeras* (fifteenth birthday celebrations for girls), documenting events with pictures, and teaching children and women (me). I also taught an adult literacy class in Xocchel for about six months until the attendees could read at a beginning level and then encouraged their children to continue working with them; all learned to read their Bibles and hymn books.

160

Soon after moving into our house, I became (by word of mouth as we got to know neighbors) our neighborhood "shot-giver," first-aid provider, I.V. applier, and health and hygiene/nutrition counselor. I also attended two births (in hammocks, which was new to me) for a neighbor woman who couldn't get to a clinic/hospital quickly enough. It, however, brings a smile to my face when I think about the second birth, as I am pretty sure it was more deliberate rather than it being an emergency and not being able to go to the clinic.

Bible studies, church planting, working with IDES (International Disaster and Emergency Services) in recovery help after several hurricanes, helping establish the *Junta Regional Juvenil* (Regional Youth Meeting) and *Culto Unido* (United Church Service), establishing the *Campamento Familiar Cristiano* (Christian Family Camp, now with a youth camp added), as well as challenges with church problems and false teachers and a split, throughout the years kept us busy, maybe too busy at times.

In the early 1990s, Polo was diagnosed with high cholesterol and given medication, which brought it down. But he didn't continue the regimen and went through ups and downs, taking medication when it went up and stopping when it came down. In the mid-90s, he began having chest pains and saw a cardiologist. Tests showed no cardiac problems, and he was diagnosed as having stress syndrome, which caused the pain. He became more irritable and moodier and had trouble sleeping. I noticed signs of sleep apnea and suggested he have that checked out, but he wouldn't. Many times, he didn't want me to go to the villages or on visits with him. His oldest brother died in an accident in November 1998 in Nuevo Laredo, Tamaulipas. After Polo returned from the funeral, his chest pains and discomfort increased, and he was obviously depressed. Finally, in January 1999, he went to our family doctor and was sent immediately to the cardiologist. Tests showed heart arrhythmia and also quite elevated cholesterol. Both doctors told him he exhibited a high-stress level and should take a break, take his medications, get a medical follow-up, and let his body heal. Our mission gave him a medical leave of absence, and he left in mid-March for the *rancho* and Monterrey.

That was the last time I saw him until 2004. He left God, church, and family behind. At times, no one in the family knew where he was. Most of the time, he lived with his youngest sister in San Antonio and worked there, and he only got intermittent medical help. After several months, our children re-established some contact with him.

The first few months after Polo left, I felt numb even as I mainly carried on with my usual activities and helped make sure preaching points were filled, supplying transportation at times. Also, I got help from the churches to plan and carry out our camp that summer. I held on to the Lord's hand and pleaded with Him for leadership and care. By the end of summer, and with Polo refusing to see or talk with me, I realized he did not plan to return. I felt angry, betrayed, and totally frustrated at that point.

When I came to the United States for family and church visits and speaking engagements in August, I saw a Christian counselor for advice as to how I should proceed. I continued to hold tight to God's hand. Right before Thanksgiving, an airline had a promotion for a new, direct flight from Mérida to San Antonio at a discounted price. So, I flew to San Antonio and went to my sister-in-law's house to talk with Polo. He wasn't there when I arrived at her house, but when he returned and saw I was there, he left without entering. My sister-in-law asked me to come and stay there instead of in a motel, so I did for the week before my return date. The whole time, Polo did not return to her house, nor did he answer a note I sent with her to work (they worked at the same place). I returned to Mérida and, after much prayer, made the decision not to try to call or see Polo again but would write occasionally. I also learned during those months that he had been unfaithful to me in our marriage and, basically, had been living a double life for several years. I felt this explained much of why he had developed stress syndrome. This discovery, however, doubled the pain I was feeling, and I threw myself into God's loving embrace for guidance, strength, and peace. Family, church (both in the States and in Yucatán), the women's English Bible study group I attended, and friends stood with me in prayer and spiritual, emotional, and moral support. Even at my lowest points, I never doubted God's presence and care. I had held back from making decisions Polo normally would make for the most part, but now God opened the door for me to begin taking on more of a leadership role in advising the church leaders when asked and helping with church plans and activities. All the congregations had men capable of preaching and teaching, who took over where Polo had been doing so. I continued to lead in camp plans and preparations while delegating more and more responsibilities to others in the church.

At the end of 1999, our largest supporting church informed me that, since a woman could not be effective alone on the field (their reason), they were reducing their support to half until June 2002 and then cutting it off. Our mission board had dropped Polo from the mission in the fall of 1999 after trying to contact him concerning his plans and receiving no response. From 2000-2002, I made several trips back to the States to report to the supporting churches and continued to trust God for needed support. We had determined when we were raising support to go to Yucatán that we would not ask for it but would present our plans and trust God to provide what we needed. He always did. I also refigured my budget to allow for me to remain on the field.

One trip was for the National Missionary Convention in November 2000. The mission board met at that time also and decided I would return to Mérida to fulfill some duties there and return to the United States in February 2001 for Homecoming at Johnson Bible College and to visit churches. I returned to Knoxville, TN, on February 19 and took Daddy to the Homecoming opening the following night. The night of the 22nd, he suffered an aortic artery aneurysm leak and had his homecoming during surgery. What a blessing to have been here with him for several weeks before returning to Mérida and to have been here when he died! (Both of Polo's parents and Mother had died while we were living in Mérida.)

The board (we were incorporated as The Way Mission) finally decided to meet in early December 2002 to decide whether to maintain the mission with me on the field as they did not want me to have financial burdens. I spent much time in prayer and had "all my ducks in a row" (reasons and plans for me to remain on the field) when I went to the meeting. But I also had prayed for God's guidance and for peace to accept whatever decision was made because I knew the board members had agonized and prayed over the situation also. They ultimately decided to close the mission, effective at the end of 2002. In retrospect, I could see God's working to mature the churches we had served so they could continue to grow autonomously.

God already had His plan set in motion, of course, and opened another door. I had stopped to visit Lisa and her two young sons in Virginia on my way to Knoxville (she was a Marine stationed at Quantico and had become a single mom). My sister-in-law's daughter from San Antonio had been living with her to help with the boys but told me she planned to stay home when she went back for Christmas, leaving Lisa with no help with her irregular work and activity hours. As soon as I got back to the house after the meeting, I called her and told her she had help with the boys if she wanted me to do so. So, I returned to Mérida for my final Christmas activities there as part of the mission and to take care of some business and pack what I could bring with me. Then, I returned to the United States to join her and her sons for the New Year of 2003. I met them at David's home in Central Islip, New York, where he and his wife (he had married one of our neighbors in the Colonia Roma in April 1995) were involved in planting a Hispanic church (they moved to Knoxville in 2005). Once we returned to Virginia, Lisa immediately applied to have me added as her dependent, and within a week, I was. That summer, she was ordered to Okinawa for three years, so off we went!

I loved Okinawa: hills that reminded me of East Tennessee, a warm climate that reminded me of Yucatán (not quite as warm), good housing and schools, many sightseeing and learning opportunities, and a church home. The only Restoration Movement congregation on the island was a non-instrumental Church of Christ. We were welcomed warmly on our first visit there (most of the congregation consisted of military members and their families, quite mobile). We became good friends with several families, friendships that continue today. Coming from such an active church life on the mission field, however, Lisa and I both felt frustrated because women were not allowed any voice in the congregation nor to participate in anything but children's classes, women's activities, and benevolent service. I did lead a women's Bible study for a few months as a fill-in, and we helped plan and carry out a VBS one summer. I also taught Spanish to one of the families for about a semester. And I became "Abuela" (grandmother) to neighbor children and helped with after-school care quite a bit. (I'd done that also in Virginia in the townhouse community where we lived.) The children heard my grandsons calling me "*Abuela*" and followed suit. I liked it because other names, such as "Mrs. Susan" or "Mrs. Calderón" (which they couldn't pronounce for the most part), sounded too stilted. At first, my grandsons were upset and complained, "You're not their *abuela*; you're ours!" I explained that these children didn't have their grandparents close by, so I could sort of substitute for them. No more complaints.

I had the privilege of taking three out-of-country trips while in Okinawa. When Lisa was deployed to Thailand with the Joint Services forces after the December 2004 tsunami, I took her place to go with her sons on a Boy Scout trip to Thailand in early 2005. As we rode through the countryside on excursions, the boys both exclaimed, "*Abuela*, this looks like Mexico!" Yes, it also reminded me of rural areas, especially in southeastern Mexico, except for the signs in Thai. We visited the Jade Buddha temple complex in Bangkok, the buildings overlaid with gold and beautiful mosaic tile work with ornate statuary everywhere. Outside the walls, beggars abounded, seeking alms, which temple attendants would confiscate most of, or the beggars would give much of to help maintain the temple complex and personnel. It broke my heart to contemplate this situation: a wall separating vast opulence from abject poverty, where all those around supported the worship of an idol, creation, instead of the Creator. It reminded me of Psalm 115:2-8:

> *Why do the nations say, "Where is their God?" Our God is in heaven; he does whatever pleases him. But their idols are silver and gold, made by human hands. They have mouths, but cannot speak, eyes, but cannot see. They have ears, but cannot hear, noses, but cannot smell. They have hands, but cannot feel, feet, but cannot walk, nor can they utter a sound with their throats. Those who make them will be like them, and so will all who trust in them.*

Thanksgiving week of 2005, we joined a Marine Corps-sponsored tour to China. What sights we saw there! When we visited the Terra Cotta Army and heard the explanation for it, I remembered Job's words (1:21), "*Naked I came from my mother's womb, and naked I will depart. The Lord gave, and the Lord has taken away; may the name of the Lord be praised.*" Also, I remembered Paul's words (1 Timothy 1:12), "*For we brought nothing into the world, and we can take nothing out of it.*" The Great Wall reminded me that nothing created can keep evil away. Only God can!

In early 2006, I had the privilege of going to Manila, in the Philippines, for a month to teach a block course in missions at the

International Christian College of Manila at the invitation of founders Ross and Cheryl Wissmann. One weekend, I went with Ross (vice president) and a team from the college to a neighboring island where a typhoon had recently swept through. We surveyed the damage and made aid plans to carry out with funds from IDES. My previous experiences in Yucatán stood us in good stead, and I served as a photographer for the group, too. One day, a faculty wife took me to Corregidor and its battle sites, including the beach site where Gen. Douglas MacArthur made his famous statement, "I shall return." He did return to help liberate the people there. That, of course, reminded me of the much greater promise of Jesus Christ in John 14:1-4:

Do not let your hearts be troubled. You believe in God; believe also in me. My Father's house has many rooms; if that were not so, would I have told you that I am going there to prepare a place for you? And if I go and prepare a place for you, I will come back and take you to be with me that you also may be where I am.

In my third week, I had the blessing of visiting Darryl and Carol Krause for a week in their work on the island of Panay. Back in Manila, we had final reviews and the final exam for the course. The Philippines and the people there made me feel quite at home with all the Spanish influence. It even has a lot of Spanish words blended into the Tagalog language, which I found fascinating. I returned in the summer of 2011 to teach two block courses, Missions and Luke (which I developed just before going) and again reveled in the culture and fellowship there.

In June 2006, my grandsons, two cats, and I flew back to Knoxville from Okinawa. Lisa had to stay for a ceremony and returned in July. I went with them back to Virginia until Thanksgiving to help them get settled in. We came to Knoxville then, and I stayed to care for my handicapped brother. My younger sister had been caring for him since Daddy died in

2001. My younger brother had begun work to place him in a supported-living home to allow us all to work. We'd been told it could take up to a year or more for Jimmy to rise to the top of the waiting list and another length of time to find an available home. God opened the door in the proceedings, and by December, Jimmy was at the top of the list and, by February of 2007, was authorized to find housing. In March, my brother and sister-in-law chose the agency through whom he would be housed (where Jimmy had attended daycare for many years) while my family and I were in Mexico for Polo's funeral.

I had never stopped loving Polo and praying for him. By God's grace, he repented and returned to Him and the church in early 2007, just a few months before he died of a massive heart attack on March 13. He was at the *rancho* on his way back to San Antonio from a visit to Yucatán. All our children and their families and I went to the *rancho* for his burial there. A preacher and his wife and two other brothers in Christ from Mérida also went there. His youngest brother, Gildardo (a Colegio Bíblico graduate who had worked with us several summers and continues to visit and help in Yucatán), and the preacher from Yucatán officiated at his burial. They gave testimony that the Word he had sown in Yucatán was still bearing fruit for the Lord.

Now, I was really alone, but only physically, for God is always with me.

In June, a house became available for Jimmy, and I began wondering what I would do next. Well, of course, God was way ahead of me with another open door. A few weeks later, I received a call from Johnson University in Knoxville, TN, asking if I would be interested in teaching Spanish there. Now, I'd never considered teaching a language, either Spanish or English. I had to laugh at God's sense of humor and tell Him that I needed His help to do so. So, I began teaching four semesters of

Spanish (two a semester) that fall and did so until graduation in 2016. What blessings I received during that experience! While at Johnson, I also had the privilege of joining a mission trip to Nicaragua with a group from a cousin's church and taking part in three Johnson-sponsored trips.

Even when we lived in Yucatán, I had wanted to get a master's degree, thinking I would do so in Spanish but not really deciding about it and not doing anything about it. When Johnson began an online master's in Intercultural Studies, that really appealed to me. After much prayer, in the fall of 2013, I registered for my first course, thinking I would take them as I could afford them, however long it took. Again, God was ahead of my game and opened a door. My dean informed me that the university had approved a full scholarship for me! Yes, I cried in joy and thanksgiving. So began another adventure for me — going back to school and doing it online. With God's constant help, I finished my studies and graduated in the spring of 2016, just before my 73rd birthday.

Meantime, in December 2015, my dean asked me if I would be interested in teaching Intercultural Studies courses at the undergraduate level once I'd graduated. I'd said yes, of course. At the beginning of 2016, the accrediting association ruled that one must have a master's in the field to teach an undergraduate course. The only Spanish I'd ever taken was the basic first-year course at Colegio Bíblico when we lived there. My dean tried to get a "grandfather" waiver to no avail. So there went my teaching Spanish. But God had an open door ready: a week after graduation, I began teaching my first online course in the School of Intercultural Studies and have taught various courses there since then and loved it. I feel that what I learned on the field in Mexico, now that I am no longer serving there, I have been able to use it to help others serve God all around the world. (One big benefit of teaching online was in allowing me to travel while teaching as long as Wi-Fi was available.) After much prayer, I ended my service at Johnson University after the spring semester of 2023. God led me during 16 wonderful years teaching there, and I miss it, but He's opening other doors for me, one of which is in producing the book of which this story will be a part.

I have been busy with other kingdom activities also. In January 2010, my family and I joined in an effort by a missionary to establish a Hispanic church here in Knoxville. We served in various capacities until the congregation was to be absorbed into the English-speaking congregation in whose facilities we worshiped in the fall of 2018. We remain active in the church where I grew up, the Christian Church of Fountain City, in Knoxville, TN. I help lead worship services and Bible studies and currently serve as Church Secretary and Assistant Treasurer. Also, I serve as a member of the planning committee of our Smoky Mountain Christian Women's Fall Getaway, held the last full weekend each September at our camp, Smoky Mountain Christian Camp in Coker Creek, TN. I served as a visiting missionary and counselor many times at the camp while still living in Mexico, and all my children and grandchildren have attended camp there, with some serving on the camp staff at times. I have been able to visit the *rancho* several times and continue to keep close contact with the brethren in Yucatán through social media and phone calls, as well as visits. Each year, I try to attend and serve in our *Campamento Familiar Cristiano*, many times leading women's workshops. I visit the churches and participate in many of their activities, as well as work with them to bring spiritual growth through teaching, rebuke, correction, and encouragement among them.

I have continued translation work, beginning in the late 1970s with articles from the *Christian Standard* and later adding Christian books. I also edit others' translations as I work with LATM (Literature and Teaching Ministries).

All my children now live in Knoxville. My daughter moved here after retiring from the Marine Corps. She bought our family home, and I live with her. All of my children participate actively in our congregation. They have given me six wonderful grandchildren. My interests include — not necessarily in order — music (most genres, both instrumental and vocal, and playing the piano and participating in singing), reading (Bible, Christian literature, suspense, historical fiction, poetry), writing poetry, Bible studies (preparing, participating, leading), family (I have six grandchildren and a grandson-in-law to love and enjoy), and travel.

Many Scriptures have served me throughout my life, but I have held Philippians 1:21 as my theme since high school – *For to me to live is Christ, and to die is gain.* Second Timothy 1:7 – *For God did not give us a spirit of cowardice but rather of power and love and self-control* – served me especially while living in Sandia Chico in difficult physical, mental, and spiritual circumstances: during difficult childbirths, dealing with situations with minimal medicines and supplies, in physical exhaustion from sleepless nights (up to several in a row), and through relationship stresses. Philippians 1:6 – *I am confident of this, that the one who began a good work in you will continue to complete it until the day of Christ Jesus* – helped sustain me for myself and especially for Polo when he fell away from Christ, and I praise God for bringing it about for him and continuing to work with me. After Polo left and I had so many decisions to make, and such a diversity of feelings, Psalm 31:15a became my strength and sustainer and has continued to fill that role to today through many decision-making and stressful times – *My times are in Your hand.* One of the more recent experiences holding on to this verse came during my master's studies. I had enrolled in two courses, understanding them to be back-to-back seven-week ones like the rest I had taken. Well, they each lasted a whole semester and covered a lot of material. Toward the latter part of the first half of the semester, it seemed I had "painted myself into a corner" because I couldn't keep up with both and make good grades in them. And I couldn't hold up under all-night sessions like when I was in college. Yes, I could have finished them with average grades, but that's not my nature. God gave me the ability to learn, and I expect to excel. I spent much time praying and decided to drop one and retake it later, even if I had to take a failing grade and redeem it, paying for it myself. The next morning, I woke up with clear guidance to talk with my dean about it. I did, and she suggested I talk with the professor of the class I planned to drop. He not only allowed me to drop but also allowed me to use any material I had already submitted if I wanted to when I re-took the course. And, as God would have it, my drop came within a few days of the cutoff date for withdrawal without failure. I gratefully went on to finish both courses well. Time and time again, when talking with someone, God has put Scriptures in my heart and mouth to handle the situations. Philippians 4:4-8, 11-21 keep me joyful, in peace, and content in life's circumstances, giving thanks always to God for His presence and care.

Rejoice in the Lord always; again I will say, rejoice! Let your gentle spirit be known to all people. The Lord is near. Do not be anxious about anything, but in everything by prayer and pleading with thanksgiving let your requests be made known to God. And the peace of God, which surpasses all comprehension, will guard your hearts and minds in Christ Jesus. Finally, brothers and sisters, whatever is true, whatever is honorable, whatever is right, whatever is pure, whatever is lovely, whatever is commendable, if there is any excellence, and if anything worthy of praise, think about these things.

Not that I speak from need, for I have learned to be content in whatever circumstances I am. I know how to get along with little, and I also know how to live in prosperity; in any and every circumstance, I have learned the secret of being filled and going hungry, both of having abundance and suffering need. I can do all things through Him who strengthens me. Nevertheless, you have done well to share with me my difficulty. You yourselves also know, Philippians, that at the first preaching of the gospel, after I left Macedonia, no church shared with me in the matter of giving and receiving except you alone, for even in Thessalonica, you sent a gift more than once for my needs. Not that I seek the gift itself, but I seek the profit which increases to your account. But I have received everything in full and have an abundance; I am amply supplied, having received from Epaphroditus what you have sent, a fragrant aroma, an acceptable sacrifice, pleasing to God. And my God will supply all your needs according to His riches in glory in Christ Jesus. Now, to our God and Father, be the glory forever and ever. Amen.

Hebrews 1:1-3 – *God, after He spoke long ago to the fathers in the prophets in many portions and in many ways, in these last days has spoken to us in His Son, whom He appointed heir of all things, through whom He also made the world,* and 2 Peter 1:3 – *for His divine power has granted to us everything pertaining to life and godliness, through the true knowledge of Him who called us by His own glory and excellence –* remind me that I need not look beyond His Word for needed wisdom and knowledge and guidance. I try to comply with these Scriptures more each day: Psalm 119:11 – *have treasured Your word in my heart, So that I may not sin against You;* Timothy 2:15 – *Be diligent to present yourself approved to God as a worker who* ¹*does not need to be ashamed, accurately handling the word of truth;* 1 Peter 3:15 – *but sanctify Christ as Lord in your hearts, always being ready to make a defense to everyone who asks you to give an account for the hope that is in you, but with gentleness and respect.*

And I look forward to the day when I can repeat with Paul 2 Timothy 4:6-8 –

For I am already being poured out as a drink offering, and the time of my departure has come. I have fought the good fight, I have finished the course, I have kept the faith; in the future there is reserved for me the crown of righteousness, which the Lord, the righteous Judge, will award to me on that day; and not only to me, but also to all who have loved His appearing.

Many events and personal encounters with others in my life could serve to provide insights for others. I will share three here, one each from my own prayer life, from wise counsel, and from another missionary's experience. (1) From when I began dating, I prayed to God that He would not allow me to maintain a romantic relationship that would lead to marriage to one He did not choose for me or if He chose for me to remain single. He granted that prayer and showed in many ways His choice of Polo as my husband (I'd already considered at that age that He wanted me to remain single and was content with that). (2) After mission trips to Mexico and Canada while at Johnson, I'd gained a much broader concept of God's mission and a deep interest in each of those countries, confusing my plan to go to Africa. I discussed this with a staff member at Johnson whom I'd known for many years and held in high regard. He listened to my confusion and told me, "You are looking to see your path ahead for a long way off. You have your open door now. Go through it, and God will open the next one. It may be to the right or the left or straight ahead, but go through it, and He will continue to open doors in His time and according to His will." When I did so, continuing my preparations to go to Africa, He directed me into the circumstances that led to my going where He had appointed for me to go — to Mexico. (3) At one of our English-speaking Bible studies in Mérida, the missionary who led them told us of an event that had made a deep impression on her spiritual life and left me with a beautiful, inspiring word picture. She and her husband were walking one night from one place to another in one of the villages. The path was uneven with rocks and roots, and no light illuminated it (how well I can picture that). Each of them had a flashlight. Her husband went ahead, using his to light down the path. She followed, using hers to illuminate each step. She told us how that brought Psalm 119:105 to mind, *Your word is a lamp to my feet and a light to my path*. As her flashlight lit the area around their feet, her husband lit the path ahead, and they could walk safely along. How wonderfully God can use events in our lives to illustrate His Word! May He continue to use me to love and serve and bless those with whom I come in contact for as long as He sees fit to keep me here on earth. And may I continue to go through the doors He opens for me until He opens the final one into His presence.

Epilogue

We have written our stories to encourage you. Perhaps you would like to write your own story. We started by answering the questionnaire that is included in the Appendices and just took off! We found that answering the questions allowed us to begin the process of writing our stories. Much thought and prayer went into developing and preparing the questionnaire. (Thank you to our Christian family counselors, Beth Ann Contreras and Judy Taylor, for their insight and contributions.) The exercise has been cathartic and meaningful in our lives. It has been a wonderful way to see how God uses situations and to see that our lives are not over – just different. We also think that many others will be blessed by doing the same exercise.

Please feel free to contact us regarding your journey, your ministry, or your life. You may reach us at <u>khera@saeministries.com</u>.

You may see yourself as "an ordinary Christian" who doesn't fulfill an extraordinary position, but, in reality, the Lord has designed His Church to be filled with members who work with one another through the Holy Spirit to bring growth to us all in love, Ephesians 4:11 – 16: *And he gave the apostles, the prophets, the evangelists, the shepherds and teachers, to equip the saints for the work of ministry, for building up the body of Christ, until we all attain to the unity of the faith and of the knowledge of the Son of God, to mature manhood, to the measure of the stature of the fullness of Christ, so that we may no longer be children, tossed to and fro by the waves and carried about by every wind of doctrine, by human cunning, by craftiness in deceitful schemes. Rather, speaking the truth in love, we are to grow up in every way into him who is the head, into Christ, from whom the whole body, joined and held together by every joint with which it is equipped, when each part is working properly, makes the body grow so that it builds itself up in love.*

May you be blessed, not forgetting the exhortation in I Thessalonians 5:16 – 18: *Rejoice always, pray without ceasing, give thanks in all circumstances; for this is the will of God in Christ Jesus for you.*

Appendix I
Questionnaire

1. What was your heart's desire for God prior to marriage?

2. How have you felt the Lord's leading in your life as a widow?

3. What is your heart's desire for God now?

4. Since the passing of your husband, are you still in ministry?

5. If so, was it necessary for you to change your ministry?

6. Considering your gifts, talents, and passions, might there be a "dream ministry" you would like to fulfill?

7. Have you thought of steps you need to take in fulfilling a "dream ministry"? Do you see the Lord leading you in that direction? If so, how?

8. Describe how your role within your family has changed and how, if at all, that is affecting your ministry.

9. Is there a circumstance where you have stepped out in faith or done something that many would consider "out of character" for you since becoming a widow? If so, how did that make you feel?

10. Name one or more circumstances where you feel the Lord has specifically used you to make a difference. Don't be modest – it is to glorify Him!

11. Since becoming a widow, do you have a sounding board, counselor, confidante, or go-to person that you feel is there for you?

Appendix II
Supportive Scriptures

Joshua 1:9

"Have I not commanded you? Be strong and courageous! Do not be terrified nor dismayed, for the LORD your God is with you wherever you go."

Psalm 1

"Blessed is the person who does not walk in the counsel of the wicked, Nor stand in the path of sinners, Nor sit in the seat of scoffers! But his delight is in the Law of the LORD, and on His Law he meditates day and night. He will be like a tree planted by streams of water, which yields its fruit in its season, and its leaf does not wither; and in whatever he does, he prospers. The wicked are not so, but they are like chaff which the wind blows away. Therefore, the wicked will not stand in the judgment, nor sinners in the assembly of the righteous. For the LORD knows the way of the righteous, but the way of the wicked will perish." (Especially v. 3)

Psalm 17:8

"Keep me as the apple of the eye; Hide me in the shadow of Your wings."

Psalm 19:7

"The Law of the LORD is perfect, restoring the soul; The testimony of the LORD is sure, making wise the simple."

Psalm 22:10-11

"I was cast upon You from birth; You have been my God from my mother's womb. Do not be far from me, for trouble is near; for there is no one to help."

Psalm 23

"The LORD is my shepherd, I will not be in need. He lets me lie down in green pastures; He leads me beside quiet waters. He restores my soul; He guides me in the paths of righteousness for the sake of His name. Even though I walk through the valley of the shadow of death, I fear no evil, for You are with me; Your rod and Your staff, they comfort me. You prepare a table before me in the presence of my enemies; You have anointed my head with oil; My cup overflows. Certainly goodness and faithfulness will follow me all the days of my life, and my dwelling will be in the house of the LORD forever." (Especially v. 4)

Psalm 25:21

"Let integrity and uprightness protect me, for I wait for You."

Psalm 27:5

"For on the day of trouble, He will conceal me in His tabernacle; He will hide me in the secret place of His tent; He will lift me up on a rock."

Psalm 31:15[a]

"My times are in Your hand."

Psalm 34:18

"The LORD is near to the brokenhearted and saves those who are crushed in spirit."

181

Psalm 39:7

"And now, Lord, for what do I wait? My hope is in You."

Psalm 100

"Shout joyfully to the LORD, all the earth. Serve the LORD with jubilation; Come before Him with rejoicing. Know that the LORD Himself is God; It is He who has made us, and not we ourselves; We are His people and the sheep of His pasture. Enter His gates with thanksgiving, and His courtyards with praise. Give thanks to Him, bless His name. For the LORD is good; His mercy is everlasting and His faithfulness is to all generations."

Psalm 119:11

"I have treasured Your word in my heart, so that I may not sin against You."

Psalm 139:16

"All the days ordained for me were written in your book before one of them came to be."

Proverbs 22:6

"Train up a child in the way he should go; even when he is old, he will not depart from it."

Isaiah 30:21

"Your ears will hear a word behind you, saying, 'This is the way, walk in it,' whenever you turn to the right or to the left."

Isaiah 41:13

"Do not fear, for I am with you; do not be afraid, for I am your God. I will strengthen you, I will also help you, I will also uphold you with My righteous right hand."

Habakkuk 3:17-19

"Even if the fig tree does not blossom, and there is no fruit on the vines, if the yield of the olive fails, and the fields produce no food, even if the flock disappears from the fold, and there are no cattle in the stalls, yet I will triumph in the LORD, I will rejoice in the God of my salvation. The Lord GOD is my strength, and He has made my feet like deer's feet, and has me walk on my high places."

Matthew 16:18

"And I also say to you that you are Peter, and upon this rock I will build My church; and the gates of Hades will not overpower it."

Matthew 28:20

"Teaching them to follow all that I commanded you; and behold, I am with you always, to the end of the age."

Luke 12:12

"For the Holy Spirit will teach you in that very hour what you ought to say."

John 14:1-4

"Do not let your hearts be troubled. You believe in God; believe also in me. My Father's house has many rooms; if that were not so, would I have told you that I am going there to prepare a place for you? And if I go and prepare a place for you, I will come back and take you to be with me that you also may be where I am."

Romans 1:16-17

"For I am not ashamed of the gospel, for it is the power of God for salvation to everyone who believes, to the Jew first and also to the Greek. For in it the righteousness of God is revealed from faith to faith; as it is written: 'BUT THE RIGHTEOUS ONE WILL LIVE BY FAITH.'"

Romans 8:28

"And we know that God causes all things to work together for good to those who love God, to those who are called according to His purpose."

Romans 10:9

"Because if you confess with your mouth that Jesus is Lord and believe in your heart that God raised him from the dead, you will be saved."

2 Corinthians 1:3-4

"Blessed be the God and Father of our Lord Jesus Christ, the Father of mercies and God of all comfort, who comforts us in all our affliction so that we will be able to comfort those who are in any affliction with the comfort with which we ourselves are comforted by God."

Philippians 1:6

"I am confident of this, that the one who began a good work in you will continue to complete it until the day of Christ Jesus."

Philippians 1:21

"For to me to live is Christ, and to die is gain."

Philippians 4:13

"I can do all things through Him who strengthens me."

Philippians 4:4-8

"Rejoice in the Lord always; again I will say, rejoice! Let your gentle spirit be known to all people. The Lord is near. Do not be anxious about anything, but in everything by prayer and pleading with thanksgiving let your requests be made known to God. And the peace of God, which surpasses all comprehension, will guard your hearts and minds in Christ Jesus. Finally, brothers and sisters, whatever is true, whatever is honorable, whatever is right, whatever is pure, whatever is lovely, whatever is commendable, if there is any excellence and if anything worthy of praise, think about these things."

Philippians 4:11-20

"Not that I speak from need, for I have learned to be content in whatever circumstances I am. I know how to get along with little, and I also know how to live in prosperity; in any and every circumstance I have learned the secret of being filled and going hungry, both of having abundance and suffering need. I can do all things through Him who strengthens me. Nevertheless, you have done well to share with me in my difficulty. You yourselves also know, Philippians, that at the first preaching of the gospel, after I left Macedonia, no church shared with me in the matter of giving and receiving except you alone; for even in Thessalonica, you sent a gift more than once for my needs. Not that I seek the gift itself, but I seek the profit which increases to your account. But I have received everything in full and have an abundance; I am amply supplied, having received from Epaphroditus what you have sent, a fragrant aroma, an acceptable sacrifice, pleasing to God. And my God will supply all your needs according to His riches in glory in Christ Jesus. Now to our God and Father be the glory forever and ever. Amen." (Especially v. 13)

1 Thessalonians 4:13-14

"But we do not want you to be uninformed, brothers and sisters, about those who are asleep, so that you will not grieve as indeed the rest of mankind do, who have no hope. For if we believe that Jesus died and rose from the dead, so also God will bring with Him those who have fallen asleep through Jesus."

1 Timothy 4:12

"Let no one look down on your youthfulness, but rather in speech, conduct, love, faith, and purity, show yourself an example of those who believe."

2 Timothy 1:7

"For God did not give us a spirit of cowardice but rather of power and love and self-control."

2 Timothy 2:15

"Be diligent to present yourself approved to God as a worker who does not need to be ashamed, accurately handling the word of truth."

2 Timothy 4:6-8

"For I am already being poured out as a drink offering, and the time of my departure has come. I have fought the good fight, I have finished the course, I have kept the faith; in the future, there is reserved for me the crown of righteousness, which the Lord, the righteous Judge, will award to me on that day; and not only to me, but also to all who have loved His appearing."

Hebrews 1:1-2

"God, after He spoke long ago to the fathers in the prophets in many portions and in many ways, in these last days has spoken to us in His Son, whom He appointed heir of all things, through whom He also made the world."

Hebrews 11:1

"Now faith is the certainty of things hoped for, a proof of things not seen."

Hebrews 13:14

"For here we do not have a lasting city, but we are seeking the city which is to come."

1 Peter 3:15

"But sanctify Christ as Lord in your hearts, always being ready to make a defense to everyone who asks you to give an account for the hope that is in you, but with gentleness and respect."

2 Peter 1:3

"For His divine power has granted to us everything pertaining to life and godliness, through the true knowledge of Him who called us by His own glory and excellence."

1 John 4:8

"The one who does not love does not know God because God is love."

3 John v. 4

"I have no greater joy than this, to hear of my children walking in the truth."

Revelation 14:13

"And I heard a voice from heaven, saying, 'Write: 'Blessed are the dead who die in the Lord from now on!'" "Yes," says the Spirit, "so that they may rest from their labors, for their deeds follow with them."

Appendix III
Checklist

No.	Category	√
1	Help to go to the grocery store	
2	Help with childcare	
3	Help with yard work.	
4	Help with cleaning the house.	
5	Help with items that are broken.	
6	Help with preparing meals.	
7	Help with paying bills and/or budgeting.	
8	Help purchasing big items - grill, car, etc.	
9	Help to find KEY people – plumber, mechanic, pest control, accountant, attorney.	
10	Help to find an area to serve in the local community.	
11	Help with laundry	
12	Help with vehicle maintenance	
13	Help establish emergency contacts	
14	Help with finances - resolving costs of the loss (funeral, medical, life insurance, health care coverage)	

No.	Category	√
15	Help with death certificate, social security, transferring or closing accounts (cable, internet, credit cards, social media, utilities, etc.)	
16	Birthday	
17	Spouse's birthday	
18	Anniversary	
19	Help to find an area to serve at church	

Appendix IV
Biblical Study on Widows

By Steve Meza

For my thoughts are not your thoughts, neither are your ways my ways, declares the Lord. For as the heavens are higher than the earth, so are my ways higher than your ways and my thoughts than your thoughts (Isaiah 55:8, 9). As all scripture is divinely inspired and useful for all things in our lives (2 Timothy 3:16, 17) and as God's view of the most vulnerable (such as widows and orphans) is different from man's, a look at these differences will lead us to a fuller understanding of His will concerning widows for followers of Jesus Christ.

The West has forgotten about widows. James wrote that *Religion that is pure and undefiled before God the Father is this: to visit orphans and widows in their affliction* (James 1:27). If this is true, then it stands to reason that a society increasingly free of religion is much more likely to neglect orphans and widows in their time of affliction. Why is James concerned about orphans and widows? And why does he expect Christians to live out their religion, at least in part, by caring for such as these? The moral relativism of our time has blurred the moral clarity necessary to answer such questions confidently, but as children of God, Christians are the privileged heirs of the moral bedrock that allows us to build a complete moral edifice with full confidence that it will withstand the test of time, intellectual scrutiny, and the innate human cry for justice. A biblical view of widows means a godly view of widows and, therefore, a clear view of widows and their place in society, in families, and in the Church.

What does moral relativism have to do with widows? And how have generational moral shifts made widows invisible in modern society? A handful of groundbreaking developments in the twentieth century combined to cloud the West's care for widows. The sexual revolution of the 1960s, easy access to birth control and abortion, no-fault divorce, well-intentioned but misguided welfare programs, and feminism have all created a world in which nearly half of new marriages end in divorce, most of them within the first ten years; additionally, an exceedingly high number of babies are born to unmarried mothers. The result is a society in which previously married women live alone, and single mothers are not only conspicuous but are often so by their own choice and, therefore, not viewed with much sympathy. To the general observer, the faithful wives of faithful men who have died are indistinguishable from the multitudes of women who divorced their husbands because they fell out of love or were abandoned by their husband for another or the countless women who became sexually active and bore children outside the love-bond of marriage.

In the absence of a biblical worldview and the abundance of personal freedom, charity, and compassion will soon die. The West is now grappling with developing a proper view of widowhood. In our culture, widowhood is often seen as little more than one of the many vicissitudes of old age, as if it could be explained entirely by the fact that men, in general, have a slightly shorter life expectancy than women (79 for women, 73 for men)[1]. But an unbiblical view of widows can and almost certainly will result in perverse treatment and abuse of one of society's most vulnerable members. Willam Carey, the nineteenth-century missionary pioneer, discovered this when he traveled to India to share the Gospel of Jesus Christ, and there he was shocked to discover the brutal practice of *sati*, the Hindu

---

[1] NATIONAL CENTER FOR HEALTH STATISTICS
NCHS Fact Sheet | March 2021.
https://www.cdc.gov/nchs/data/factsheets/factsheet_nvss.pdf

tradition of burning the wife with her dead husband on his funeral pyre because she was considered to be responsible for his death[2].

Cultural views on widowhood are a powerful force and one difficult to change. Even in Israelite culture, widowhood was seen as a punishment from God. When Naomi returned to Israel after the death of her husband and two sons, the reaction of the Israelite community and her response to them is very revealing, *So the two of them went on until they came to Bethlehem. And when they came to Bethlehem, the whole town was stirred because of them. And the women said, "Is this Naomi?" She said to them, "Do not call me Naomi; call me Mara, for the Almighty has dealt very bitterly with me. I went away full, and the LORD has brought me back empty. Why call me Naomi when the LORD has testified against me and the Almighty has brought calamity upon me?"* (Ruth 1:19-20). This is why we do well to remember, to paraphrase Old Testament Scholar Katie McCoy, that God did not create a culture; he *entered* a culture. Israelites already had their own views of widows, which informed their treatment of them, one that God repeatedly spoke against and commanded to be replaced with his own view of them.

In ancient times, widows were easy prey in a male-dominated society. In many cultures, including Israel, women did not have inheritance rights, aside from rare exceptions (Num. 27:3-7). The livelihood and safety of women were almost always tied to a male relative, ideally a husband. But when a husband died, a widow became instantly a vulnerable member of society. Therefore, God explicitly commanded that widows were to be seen as a protected class in society. In Exodus 22:22, it is plainly stated, *You shall not mistreat any widow or fatherless child.* Moreover, the commandment is followed by a curse on anyone who violates the law, *If you do mistreat*

---

[2] Crossman, meg. "Pioneers of the Movement." *Pathways to Global Understanding.* Pg. 134. Seattle: YWAM Publishing. 2003

[widows], and they cry out to me, I will surely hear their cry, and my wrath will burn, and I will kill you with the sword, and your wives shall become widows and your children fatherless. In this case, widowhood is indeed a judgment from God, but not against the widow, but rather against her evil husband for his own abuse of widows.

God is portrayed in the Old Testament as the protector of widows. David describes God as worthy of praise precisely because he appointed himself to be "Father of the fatherless and protector of widows is God in his holy habitation." (Psalms 68:5). He puts oppressors on notice that "He executes justice for the fatherless and the widow" (Deuteronomy 10:18), and he reassures them through Jeremiah 49:11, *Leave your fatherless children; I will keep them alive; and let your widows trust in me.* Widows, orphans, and sojourners are often grouped together as the most vulnerable members of society and whose cause God takes on their behalf. They are loved and cared for by God, and those who abuse and exploit them will have to answer for this especially egregious form of evil to God himself, who will restore to them their dignity.

But the immediate responsibility of caring for widows belongs to men. It is good for our culture to begin to see widows as beloved by God and seen by him with approval and concern, but it is not enough. As James writes concerning the transfer of ideas into action, *What good is it, my brothers, if someone says he has faith but does not have works? Can that faith save him?*(James 2:14) More specifically, he points to the care for widows and orphans as a sign of true religion (James 1:27). The community at large is to make provision for the defenseless, this is the purpose behind this commandment in Deuteronomy 24:19, *When you reap your harvest in your field and forget a sheaf in the field, you shall not go back to get it. It shall be for the sojourner, the fatherless, and the widow, that the LORD your God may bless you in all the work of your hands.* Boaz's faithful obedience to this law played a role that is impossible to overestimate in the life of one of the Bible's most famous widows, Ruth. Ruth encountered Boaz precisely because she was a widow collecting the gleanings of Boaz's field. Far from seeing her with contempt, Boaz recognized that Ruth was noble and a woman of virtue (Ruth 2:10-13). The story ends with the marriage of Boaz and Ruth and the birth of their son, Obed. But it is not lost on Matthew that the birth of the Messiah himself runs through the providential encounter of a young widow and an Israelite man with a biblical view of widows (Matthew 1:1-6).

The story of Ruth emphasizes the broad responsibility of society toward widows, but it also alludes to a much more direct and personal provision for men's care for widows, or *a* man's care for *a* widow, to be more precise. Mosaic Law instituted Levirate *marriage*, which required the brother of a dead man to marry his sister-in-law, particularly if the husband had died without descendants. In starkest contrast with the Hindu practice of sati mentioned above, in which widows were burned with their husbands, Israelites married widows to their brother-in-law. Deuteronomy 25:5-10 states, *"If brothers dwell together, and one of them dies and has no son, the wife of the dead man shall not be married outside the family to a stranger. Her husband's brother shall go into her and take her as his wife and perform the duty of a husband's brother to her. And the first son whom she bears shall succeed to the name of his dead brother, that his name may not be blotted out of Israel. And if the man does not wish to take his brother's wife, then his brother's wife shall go up to the gate to the elders and say, 'My husband's brother refuses to perpetuate his brother's name in Israel; he will not perform the duty of a husband's brother to me.' Then the elders of his city shall call him and speak to him, and if he persists, saying, 'I do not wish to take her,' then his brother's wife shall go up to him in the presence of the elders and pull his sandal off his foot and spit in his face. And she shall answer and say, 'So shall it be done to the man who does not build up his brother's house.' And the name of his house shall be called in Israel, 'The house of him who had his sandal pulled off.'* To modern readers, this might not seem like a desirable situation

195

for women, but we must understand that this provision was intended to secure property and provide protection and security for widows. Indeed, even before this practice was codified into law, it was expected and demanded by women like Tamar demanded of Judah, the patriarch (Gen. 38:8-26). In the case of Tamar in Genesis, as well as the law in Deuteronomy, the widow was considered the injured party if the levirate law was violated, and it was her complaint that prompted legal action against the derelict brother-in-law. However one might feel about such a commandment and its implementation, what is essential to understand is that God's commandment is two-fold. First, widows are not to be discarded, neglected, or unjustly held liable for the death of their husbands; rather, they deserve consideration and full access to a fulfilling life. Secondly, God considers a marriage dissolved when a spouse dies, and therefore, widows have a legitimate right to be married again, not confined to a life of solitude and loneliness.

In the New Testament, widows are usually portrayed in a sympathetic light, but also against the backdrop of a society that has failed to properly care for them. Jesus praised the widow who gave two copper coins (Mark 12:42-44; Luke 21:2-3). While her offering had very little economic value, as a percentage of people's gifts, she gave all she had, while others gave only a fraction. Some have observed, however, that more than a statement about her generosity, the narrative points out that she was living in an exploitative environment that not only did not provide for her but also demanded what little she had! Jesus felt compassion for the widow of Nain and raised her only son from the dead (Luke 7:11-17); he openly called out the Scribes who exploited vulnerable widows (Mark 12:38-44), and this attitude was carried into the early church by the Apostles (Acts 6:1-6). Paul wrote to Timothy that widows are to be treated with honor; however, not all widows are the same, for those who have children and grandchildren, in other words, who have family to lean on, should be the responsibility of their family. But some widows have no one to depend on, and they should receive support from the church (1 Timothy 5:3-16). Widows are not obligated to re-marry but are allowed to and even encouraged to do so if they are young and unable to remain sexually pure (1 Corinthians 7:8-9).

The Bible has very little to say about men whose wives have died. There are no specific commandments nor compelling stories about widowers. But God has spoken often and with great intensity about widows and their role in society, society's obligations toward them, and especially the Church's duty to them. In his ministry, Jesus demonstrated the same compassion and honor for widows that characterize the God of the Old Testament, and his Apostles bequeathed that value to every generation of disciples thereafter. A biblical view of widowhood, therefore, recognizes that the singleness of widows is of a different kind than that of women who have been divorced or never married, that her vulnerability is similar to that of orphans and foreigners, that even her very widowhood is different from that of men's; but that God has a particular love for them, which is necessarily manifested materially through the Church, which is the body of Christ, his Son

Made in the USA
Columbia, SC
19 February 2024